# Suffragism and the Great War

# Suffragism and the Great War

Vivien Newman

Pen & Sword
**MILITARY**

First published in Great Britain in 2018 by
PEN & SWORD MILITARY
An imprint of
Pen & Sword Books Ltd
Yorkshire - Philadelphia

ISBN 978 1 52671 897 6

Typeset in INDIA by Geniies IT & Services Private Limited
Printed and bound by TJ International Ltd, Padstow, Cornwall

Pen & Sword Books Ltd incorporates the Imprints of Aviation, Atlas, Family History, Fiction, Maritime, Military, Discovery, Politics, History, Archaeology, Select, Wharncliffe Local History, Wharncliffe True Crime, Military Classics, Wharncliffe Transport, Leo Cooper, The Praetorian Press, Remember When, Seaforth Publishing and Frontline Publishing.

For a complete list of Pen & Sword titles please contact
PEN & SWORD BOOKS LTD
47 Church Street, Barnsley, South Yorkshire, S70 2AS, England
E-mail: enquiries@pen-and-sword.co.uk
Website: www.pen-and-sword.co.uk

Or

PEN AND SWORD BOOKS
1950 Lawrence Rd, Havertown, PA 19083, USA
E-mail: Uspen-and-sword@casematepublishers.com
Website: www.penandswordbooks.com

*This book is for my daughters Rosalind and Elizabeth-Ann. They, like me, were first introduced to voting by their 'grand-nan', Irene Turtle. She took us all at very young ages into the polling booth and explained the importance of that firmly pencilled X for which women had fought so hard during her lifetime. This book is dedicated to her memory.*

# Acknowledgements

My thanks once again to my editor Karyn Burnham. Her eagle eye and apposite comments have removed a number of errors. Any that remain are of course my own.

As always, my husband Ivan has been fully committed to this project. His admiration for these remarkable women on all sides of the suffrage divide is only surpassed by my own.

# Acronyms

| | |
|---|---|
| AFL | Actresses' Franchise League |
| ASL | Anti-Suffrage League |
| *BMJ* | *British Medical Journal* |
| CLWS | Church League for Women's Suffrage |
| COs | Conscientious Objectors (also referred to as Conchies) |
| ELFS | East London Federation for Women's Suffrage |
| IWSA | International Women's Suffrage Alliance |
| JWF | Joint Women's Franchise |
| LCSWS | London Central Society for Women's Suffrage |
| MLOWS | Men's League for Opposing Women's Suffrage |
| NVA | National Vigilance Association |
| NCF | No-Conscription Fellowship |
| NUSEC | National Union of Societies for Equal Citizenship |
| NUWSS | National Union of Women's Suffrage Societies |
| PES | Passmore Edwards Settlement |
| QMAAC | Queen Mary's Auxiliary Army Corps (formerly WAAC) |
| RAMC | Royal Army Medical Corps |
| RASC | Royal Army Service Corps |
| SOSBW | Society for Overseas Settlement of British Women |
| SWH | Scottish Women's Hospitals for Foreign Service |
| TRL | Tax Resistance League |

| | |
|---|---|
| WAAC | Women's Auxiliary Army Corps (became QMAAC) |
| WEC | Women's Emergency Corps |
| WFL | Women's Freedom League |
| WHC | Women's Hospital Corps |
| WILPF | Women's International League for Peace and Freedom |
| WL | Women's Legion |
| WLA | Women's Land Army |
| WPS | Women's Police Service |
| WPV | Women's Police Volunteers |
| WRAF | Women's Royal Air Force |
| WSPU | Women's Social and Political Union |
| WVR | Women's Volunteer Reserve |
| WWAC | Women's War Agriculture Committee |
| YMCA | Young Men's Christian Association |

# Contents

## Chapter One

# 'Getting ready to fight a bigger battle'

## 'Lord Curzon is up, Ladies. But 'e won't do you no 'arm'[1]

On 10 January 1918, a group of women were anxiously waiting in a House of Lords' Committee Room. Lord Curzon, former Viceroy of India, President of the Anti-Suffrage League and Leader of their Lordships' House, had risen to his feet to wind up the debate on the latest Representation of the People Act. After five decades of struggling for the vote, 70-year-old Millicent Fawcett, President of the National Union of Women's Suffrage Societies (NUWSS) was far from complacent. She had calculated that at least seven lords, including the all-important Curzon, remained opposed to enfranchising women. Sitting beside her was an equally worried Mary Ward, committed anti-suffragist. Both women knew that much depended on which way Curzon led the debate.[2] Would he remain true to his anti-suffrage beliefs or would he finally, as one policeman assured the waiting women, do suffragism 'no 'arm'.

To Mary's ears, Curzon opened encouragingly, rehearsing the well-worn anti-suffrage arguments and affirming that 'his mistrust and apprehension were as great as they had ever been'; then he changed tack. Unwilling to 'take upon himself the responsibility of "precipitating a conflict from which your lordships would not emerge with credit"', he would abstain.[3] In the division that followed 134 Lords and Bishops (including both Archbishops) voted in favour of women's enfranchisement, seventy-one against, thirteen abstained. The policeman had been right. Anti-suffrage MP Arnold Ward was 'white in the face with rage as he heard Curzon's pompous treachery', whilst his dismayed sister Dorothy recorded in her diary, 'We have been betrayed by our leader Lord Curzon. Coward!'[4] Their mother Mary begged Millicent, her long-time opponent, to support her in 'trying to get [the Bill] submitted to a referendum'.[5] Explaining Prime Minister Lloyd George's view that a referendum was 'an expensive method of denying justice',

Millicent refused, leaving the Wards to wend their disconsolate way home, 'on the only available vehicle, a number 11 bus'.[6]

Although for both Millicent and Mary this was an historic day, other women, such as auxiliary nurse Vera Brittain serving with the Red Cross in Etaples, France, remembered being, 'completely unaware that … the Representation of the People Bill, which gave votes to women over the age of thirty, had been passed by the House of Lords'. For Vera, 'the spectacular pageant of the woman's movement' had 'crept to its quiet, unadvertised triumph in the deepest night of wartime depression'.[7]

The struggle for women's parliamentary enfranchisement had been long and bitter. Women had locked horns and multiple suffrage societies had developed, some with limited, others with wide membership. The women who became known, courtesy of Charles Hands in the 10 January 1906 *Daily Mail,* as the 'suffragettes' had fought for the vote through militant, at times violent campaigns (although care was taken to ensure lives were not endangered). They had been imprisoned, undertaken hunger and thirst strikes, and, following King Edward VII's 13 August 1909 suggestion to Home Secretary Herbert Gladstone, suffered the torture of forcible feeding. Non-militant or constitutional suffragists had used legal, non-violent and passive resistance to demonstrate that women were as worthy of enfranchisement as the two out of three men aged over 21 who now enjoyed the right to vote. It seemed at times to both suffragettes and suffragists that Victory would forever elude them.

### The pre-war Suffrage Story: this 'mad wicked folly of "Women's Rights"'.[8]

Writing about the rise of the suffrage movement, Dr Mary Gordon, the first female inspector of prisons who had herself worked at Holloway, commented, 'we do not know how it sprang to life, no one explanation is entirely satisfactory … It began all over the country in silent, lonely places … it was not premeditated or controllable – it *happened*' during the 1860s, a decade when of the 10,380,258 women of all ages resident in England and Wales, 2,293,752 were either spinsters or widows.[9] Once started, women's thirst for political rights seemed unquenchable but the road proved long and weary and the struggle harsher than many anticipated.

In November 1913, Edmund Turner noted how, in the Middle Ages and the early modern period, women had not been excluded from the body politic. Indeed 'tenure and service rather than persons furnished the basis of organisation, and instances occur of women taking part in local affairs and holding office and jurisdiction'.[10] Whilst acknowledging that few women held positions that allowed them to hold 'office and jurisdiction' they had, over the centuries, become excluded from the political process. Even in the mid-seventeenth century, politically aware women had lobbied parliament; in *Vindication of the Rights of Women* (1792), Mary Wollstonecraft asserted that even if 'I may excite laughter, … I really think that women ought to have representatives, instead of being arbitrarily governed.'[11] In 1792, it was not only women who were unrepresented in Parliament, however. The First Reform Act (1832) widened the male franchise and excluded women by explicitly using the term 'male person'. As married women's interests were supposedly represented by their husbands and unmarried women's by their fathers they had, so the argument went and would continue to go, no need of the vote. In 1866, having already touched upon female suffrage in his election address, Liberal MP John Stuart Mill presented a petition, signed by 1,499 women, requesting the enfranchisement of 'all householders without distinction of sex, who possess such property or rental qualification as your Honourable House may determine'.[12] (This excluded married women as they could not be householders.) The spectators as this petition was presented included Millicent Garrett. Better known as Millicent Fawcett, her constitutional suffrage story spans all campaigns between 1866 and 1918. In 2018, she will finally take her rightful place alongside Winston Churchill and Nelson Mandela when her statue is unveiled in Parliament Square.

Following his abortive 1866 foray into female representation, Mill unsuccessfully strove to move an amendment to the 1867 Second Reform Act: the word 'person' should replace the term 'male person'. For the next seventeen years, all attempts to extend the franchise to at least unmarried women were defeated, some more conclusively than others. Meanwhile women formed numerous suffrage societies with membership drawn from across the country and from all social classes; some societies aligned themselves with political parties or potential and current MPs who pronounced themselves in favour of at least limited women's suffrage. The

London National Society for Women's Suffrage was formed in July 1867, Manchester and Edinburgh societies soon followed.[13] By 1914 the suffrage movement counted at least fifty-six separate societies with a combined membership of over 300,000 women many of whom became hardened campaigners, not on the field of battle but as veterans of a war fought against (primarily but far from exclusively) male prejudice.

Despite the proliferation of societies, by 1892 even the most optimistic of supporters must have struggled to remain hopeful. Liberal Prime Minister William Gladstone and Home Secretary Herbert Asquith vehemently opposed the idea of enfranchising women. Writing to MP Samuel Smith, Gladstone confessed 'the fear I have is, lest we should invite her to trespass upon the delicacy, the purity, the refinement, the elevation of her own nature'.[14] By declaring his opposition, he made female suffrage an issue of party loyalty, an action that left several pro-suffrage MPs, including Millicent Fawcett's husband, Henry – a Liberal Cabinet Member, in a cleft stick: listen to their conscience or defy their party. Not all found this easy to resolve. Gladstone and other MPs' views that women were too delicate to put an X on a ballot paper appears deeply hypocritical in the light of the Liberal and indeed all political parties' dependence on their female auxiliary organisations for canvassing, fundraising and election work. Diarist Kate Frye cynically commented how in 1907 (the Liberals) 'wanted the Liberal Women's help to get into the House and now they don't care two straws'.[15] The Conservative Party's Primrose League estimated its 1891 membership at around half a million women and the Women's Liberal Federation had 82,000 members in 1896.[16] Familiarity with canvassing, lobbying and raising their own profile would stand many women in good stead during the their own suffrage campaigns and subsequently during the war.

If the 1894 Local Government Act had given some women the right to vote and stand in local elections, parliamentary representation remained a distant dream. In 1896 at a meeting presided over by the now widowed Millicent Fawcett, some seventeen suffrage societies saw the benefit of working together, in October 1897 they amalgamated into the National Union of Women's Suffrage Societies (NUWSS). They would remain committed to campaigning for the vote through constitutional means including numerous petitions; one in the mid-1890s garnered more than 257,000 signatures, whilst in December 1910 hundreds of thousands of male voters also signed their support of women's enfranchisement.[17] Highly visible, eye-catching activities such as pageants and processions kept women's suffrage in the public eye. Despite her conviction that the militant Women's Social and Political Union (WSPU) was inflicting serious damage on the women's cause, Millicent with her superb leadership skills and her 'flair for conciliation spiced with dry wit', remained adamant that women who held different views should not turn on each other and she even organised a celebratory banquet in December 1906 for the militant women just released from Holloway.[18] Many NUWSS members would demonstrate and use similar skills to further suffragists' contribution to the war effort.

Whilst the NUWSS were campaigning constitutionally, the same cannot be said of all suffrage groups. The Pankhurst family, Emmeline, Christabel and Sylvia, were becoming ever more frustrated by the lack of progress; they were also disappointed by the Independent Labour Party's increasingly half-hearted support for the women's cause. In October 1903, they took a step that would have significant ramifications and turn Pankhurst into a household name – revered or vilified by thousands. Emmeline founded the WSPU in Manchester, moving its Headquarters to Clements Inn, London, to be nearer the seat of power in October 1906, with the initial aim of obtaining votes for women on the same terms as men. Operating under the slogan 'Deeds not Words', the Pankhursts and their acolytes' deeds would rock British society to its very foundations as they pursued their ever more dramatically anti-government, militant policies. Opinions on the Pankhursts were (and remain) polarised. Some considered Emmeline, 'the most remarkable political and social agitator of the twentieth century and the supreme protagonist of the campaign for the electoral enfranchisement of women.'[19] Others argue that she contributed to Prime Minister Asquith's continuing vehement objections and thus delayed female suffrage. On 14 December 1911, following the tragic events of 'Black Friday' (see Chapter Three), Asquith assured an Anti-Suffrage deputation that female enfranchisement would be 'a political mistake of a very disastrous kind'.[20] Unlike many parliamentarians, Asquith's views never really changed although at the end of the war he paid lip service to female enfranchisement. Having lost his parliamentary seat in the December 1918 election, in a 1920 speech in Paisley, he damned women voters as a 'dim, impenetrable lot, for the most part, hopelessly ignorant of politics, credulous to the last degree and flickering with gusts of sentiment like a candle in the wind'.

Although there were very significant differences between the NUWSS and the WSPU's methods and these differences became increasingly pronounced as militancy escalated, their ideological similarities were pronounced. Significantly for future wartime work, the organisations shared a heightened gender consciousness, believing that only the vote would end the centuries-long sexual exploitation of women; these beliefs led to increased contact between the social classes. Although the WSPU would latterly become largely associated with middle- or even upper-class women, it retained a strong core of working-class women supporters. An ability to work with women from different classes would prove useful during the war as, at times, those from the most privileged ranks of society would find themselves working close to women who had not enjoyed the benefits of rank and money.

Following a deep rift in 1907 caused by Emmeline Pankhurst's increasingly autocratic leadership, Sylvia Pankhurst and the elderly Charlotte Despard (sister to the first wartime commander of the British Expeditionary Force, Sir John French) formed the Women's Freedom League (WFL) which worked extensively amongst the poorest of the poor in the East End of London where they then both lived. Advocating militancy, both were imprisoned for their actions, Sylvia on numerous occasions and Charlotte on fewer than she would have liked. They remained committed to universal female enfranchisement as opposed to only enfranchising women from more privileged social classes upon whom the WSPU's attention was increasingly focused.

By 1914 there were more than 500 NUWSS branches with 50,000 members across the country.[21] The WSPU was always secretive about its membership but by February 1909 its magazine *Votes for Women* had a circulation of 16,000 and in the year from February 1908 to February 1909 WSPU income had virtually tripled to over £21,000 (over £2,000,000 today), however new membership declined from 1909 onwards.[22] At its peak, the WSPU had eighty-eight branches, largely in London and the Southeast.[23]

Whilst thousands of women and indeed men (there were many men's suffrage leagues amongst all groups other than the WSPU which eventually 'expelled' male members), not to mention a significant number of MPs who were either actively campaigning for the vote or at least supporting the idea between 1867 and 1914, one group of women as well as men were actively working with the opposite aim in mind.[24] In June 1889, an Appeal Against Female Suffrage was launched and signed by many titled and upper-class women as well as some with distinguished records in academia, philanthropy and public service. Other signatories were members of the middle class who, thanks to inherited money and their own talents, never 'experienced the disadvantages many women faced'.[25] Anti-suffragism was largely built on the conviction that the 'pursuit of mere outward equality with men was for women not only vain but demoralising'.[26] The journal 'The Nineteenth Century' argued that the pursuit of equality 'leads to a total misconception of woman's true dignity and special mission'.[27] Although individual women changed sides, the Anti-Suffrage League (ASL) never altered its position on women's enfranchisement.

Before the war both pros and antis tried to gain press coverage of their activities (the WSPU leadership remained unperturbed by the frequently negative publicity). The NUWSS and the WSPU ran efficient press departments, subscribing to cutting agencies, liaised with press agencies and placed articles by their members in journals and newspapers. To try to increase public awareness of non-militant suffragism, the London Central Society for Women's Suffrage (LCSWS) had thirty-three press secretaries within its sixty-one constituencies; at least some of these women would have continued in similar roles during the war. Suffrage women's wartime activities were now of greater interest to the press than the pre-war activities of constitutional suffragists (as opposed to suffragettes). If in 1912 'one woman breaking a window could make all England ring', one woman killed or wounded by the so-called barbarous Hun could make all England weep with fury.[28]

The NUWSS and especially the Committee behind the wartime Scottish Women's Hospital Units for Foreign Service (SWH) proved particularly adept at feeding the press accounts and photographs of groups of SWH members on Active Service. They frequently feature in the suffrage-supporting *British Journal of Nursing* as well as the NUWSS' own *Common Cause*. One SWH member cynically commented that the hardships and dangers they endured always looked good in the papers.

Whilst most pro-suffrage societies and organisations at least partially suspended their activities during hostilities and poured their energies into the war effort, the Anti-Suffrage League remained committed in its opposition, aware that the tide was turning against them. If in June 1914 Lord Curzon had been able to announce confidently at the League's Annual Meeting, 'I think that we may say that the cause of women's votes is absolutely dead in the present House of Commons', by 1916, most anti-suffragists knew in their hearts that they had lost the intellectual debate and the position which Curzon had recently considered to be secure was now untenable. Far from Curzon's abstention from voting against the January 1918 Representation of the People Bill in the House of Lords being the cowardly act of which Dorothy Ward accused him, it was that of a pragmatic leader deeply conscious of Parliament's mood.

## 'Public Demonstrations of Faith':[29] The Spectacle of Women.

Marches including women's marches, sometimes attended by hundreds of thousands of protesters, are now part of the everyday, democratic fabric of our lives. An estimated 470,000 (predominantly) women attended the January 2017 Women's March in Washington which overshadowed President Trump's first day in office.[30] It is now hard to comprehend the enormity of the step when, in 1907, women first took to the streets in public marches to promote and draw attention to their ardent belief in female enfranchisement.

Designed to demonstrate the depth of support for women's suffrage, timed to coincide with the opening of Parliament and now known for obvious reasons as the 'Mud March', the first women's march took place on 9 February 1907. With 'long skirts trailing in the mud [and] hearts in which enthusiasm struggled successfully with propriety', some 3,000 women wended their way from Hyde Park Corner to Exeter Hall in the Joint Women's Franchise Demonstration United Procession of Women.[31] 'In that year the vast majority of women still felt that there was something very dreadful in walking in procession through the streets ... many of the demonstrators felt that they were risking their employments and endangering their reputations'; they anticipated 'public ridicule and shame'.[32] But far from greeting the marchers with ridicule, thousands of Londoners braved the rain to watch women from all strata of society march together and, much to the organisers' and marchers' satisfaction, the event received wide coverage in both the European and American press.

Kate Frye (who eventually became a paid employee helping to run the LCSWS workshop employing dressmakers made redundant by the war) realised, 'We were an imposing spectacle all with badges – each section under its own banner … I felt like a martyr of old and walked proudly along.'[33] Kate's excitement at having participated in this epoch-marking event remains palpable a century later. This was many women's first, but far from last, heady experience of marching shoulder to shoulder, rendering themselves highly visible in a public space; pride in their actions stayed with many participants as it did with most subsequent marchers. The Mud March, which forced the public to take notice of the depth of support for Votes for Women, was the forerunner of countless such pre-war events. Kate's appetite was whetted and she attended and subsequently wrote in detail about several marches. Like all future marches, pageants and processions (and the 1915 'Right to Serve March'), the Mud March brought together women of all classes and backgrounds: titled ladies, university students, working class women, tax resisters, ex-prisoners marched proudly together holding banners aloft – frequently the group rewarded with the loudest cheers were the women marching under the Prisoners' Banner. Women who marched in processions highlighting women's work and achievements during the Great War reported similar euphoria.

1907 was the first of the 'Marching Years' though, after the experiences of the Mud March, organisers wisely avoided large-scale marches in the winter months. Just as wartime marchers would process in uniform, leaders advised suffragists to wear their societies' colours: amongst many others, the WSPU's purple, white and green, the white, green and red of the NUWSS, the black, white and grey of the Tax Resisters' League; women marched under diverse banners such as 'Actresses' Franchise League' and 'Office Staff N.W.S.P.U'.[34] Many department stores cannily marketed appropriate 'costumes' that more affluent women could purchase for their marches. This trend continued during the war, thus Harrods 'specialise[d] in Outfits for every type of war-activity'. Instructions issued to marchers in *Votes for Women* 9 June 1911 include 'wear white if possible with a gay display of colours; wear a gown that clears the ground; wear a small hat'. An image of 'Suffragettes "forming up" in the Prisoners' Pageant of the

Women's Coronation Procession held on 17 June 1911' indicates that they had complied.[35]

As well as keeping women's enfranchisement in the public eye, marches proved useful recruiting grounds. Liberal MP David Thomas's daughter, Margaret Mackworth, Viscountess Rhondda and an important First World War women's leader, enrolled in the militant WSPU after participating in the 21 July 1908 march. A month away from being married, she had some, although 'not very much difficulty in persuading' her future husband that (marching) was acceptable.[36] Her pro-suffrage mother accompanied her 'because she did not think that an unmarried girl should walk unchaperoned through the gutter'.[37] Margaret enjoyed herself but 'mother did not as she came of a generation that took the gutter and casual insults hard'.[38] Soon both women would be performing far more dastardly actions than marching, either in or out of the gutter, and both, like her mother's close friend Florence Haig, a relative of wartime commander Sir Douglas Haig, would spend time in prison. In May 1915, Margaret walking in an unladylike fashion in the gutter would have been the least of her mother's worries; Margaret was feared drowned following the torpedoing of the *Lusitania*.

On 22 June 1911, George V was to be crowned King Emperor with all the pomp and ceremony – and male dominated processions – at which Britain (still) excels. To draw attention to His Majesty's female subjects' multiple contributions to national life, the WSPU, the WFL and the NUWSS joined forces and, working with a wide range of smaller societies, brought militants and constitutionalists together in one grand, consciousness-raising, eye-catching display: the 17 June 1911 Suffrage Coronation Procession. Boasting, according to one of the advertising flyers, '70 bands, 1,000 banners and being 5 miles long', there was ample opportunity for it to be, as 5 May 1911 *Votes for Women* promised, 'not only National in its character but also Imperial and International'. If the pictures and press accounts are to be believed, it was certainly spectacular for as well as contingents from the United Kingdom 'home countries', there were banners and floats representing all the King's Dominions. Present, or at least represented, were suffrage supporters from far-flung lands and territories, some of whom, such as the Australian and New Zealand representatives, already enjoyed the vote and others who would have to wait for long after British women were enfranchised. In a 1908 NUWSS march, the Australia and New Zealand Women Voters Association's banner depicted a daughter figure, 'Commonwealth of Australia', addressing Mother Britannia with the message, 'Trust the women, Mother, as I have done', alluding to the fact that Australian women had been enfranchised in 1902.[39] Some of these overseas women who marched shoulder to shoulder with their British sisters would return a few years later this time 'On Active Service Overseas'.

The Women's Coronation Procession included 'notable women from the past' and a smattering of saints or, at least in the case of Joan of Arc, a saint-to-be.[40] The idea of using women saints which occurred in both pageants and processions was one that the Women's Military Hospital Endell Street copied a few years later. As wards in Military Hospitals were denoted by letters of the alphabet, former WSPU members doctors Flora Murray and Louisa Garrett Anderson (Millicent Fawcett's niece) named each ward alphabetically after a female saint. St Onorio caused some subsequent embarrassment. The patron saint of wet nurses, she was not someone wounded soldiers needed to invoke.

The Coronation Procession was the last great joint march. In December 1911 Asquith told an anti-suffrage demonstration that enfranchising women 'would be a political mistake of a very disastrous kind'; in early 1912, Emmeline Pankhurst ordered an intensification of destructive militancy. Violence and imprisonments escalated; open-air WSPU meetings were banned in April 1913, it seemed that the public would no longer be entertained by WSPU marches and processions although the NUWSS would soon be planning what turned out to be a final spectacular pre-war event although, unexpectedly, the war would bring WSPU procession coordinators back into the limelight.

## A Pageant of Great Women.

In 1905 a craze began in the small Dorset town of Sherborne which would soon sweep the land and be exploited by suffrage societies; pageants soon attracted hundreds, even thousands, of spectators.[41] Unsurprisingly, suffrage leaders set about exploiting such popularity and organised a pageant focusing on historical women, some such as Florence Nightingale enjoyed world renown, others were simply role models and inspirational women who had contributed to or enriched public life. Although most pageants were semi-static open-air ones, Actresses' Franchise League member Cicely Hamilton devised an alternative one. In November 1909, a *Pageant of Great Women* opened at London's Scala Theatre; it subsequently toured the country and featured some fifty suffrage women (including actress Ellen Terry), dressed up as artists, saintly women, heroic women and warriors. Herself a major general's daughter, Cicely portrayed (Mrs) Christian Davies who fought in Marlborough's army at Blenheim and Ramillies. Kenyon Musgrove, assumedly a suffrage supporter, played the only male, part, 'Prejudice'.[42] A book version of the play was sold through the Suffrage Shop, presumably as a fundraiser, as indeed the opening performance had been.

Emmeline Pethwick-Lawrence, an ardent WSPU member, at least until she was ousted by 'generalissimo' Emmeline Pankhurst, favoured pageants and processions over petitions:

> Petitions go into parliamentary wastepaper baskets. They cannot put a procession of fifteen thousand women into waste-paper bins. ... All London comes out to see them and those that see the amazing spectacle of two miles of women, women of every class, of every profession, and every calling – realise perfectly well that they represent a very great and widespread and irresistible demand.[43]

Between 1909 and 1913, suffragists found compelling methods of dramatizing their cause. They used visual arts with beautiful banners worked by members of the Artists' Suffrage League, whilst performance and public entertainment earned unprecedented essential press coverage of their activities. The new popular daily press had a voracious appetite for spectacle and this more than anything gave the oxygen of publicity to the suffrage processions, pageants and the 1913 pilgrimage.[44] Women were learning lessons about exploiting the media and appealing to readers. Suffrage leaders, who frequently became wartime ones, fully understood the need to court the press which could and did mould public opinion.

## 'Holy Pilgrims, Brazen Hussies'.

Although processions were the most obvious way in which thousands of women came together to increase public awareness of and press interest in their cause, in 1913, the NUWSS felt that with the suffragettes once again embarked on an increasingly unpopular militancy campaign, it behoved them to create a very different spectacle of women. This would not be the spectacle of women breaking shop windows, committing arson and setting fire to pillar boxes but a public demonstration of law-abiding women with an added spiritual undertone. With close on 100,000 members, they would promote peaceful, constitutional suffragism. On 18 April Katherine Harley, whom Millicent considered the 'the life and soul of the suffrage movement' in Shrewsbury, a woman 'of great originality and imagination', proposed the idea of a women's pilgrimage.[45] Spirituality would provide a useful counterpoint to WSPU militancy.

Organised with 'exemplary speed made possible by the smooth-running system of federations that was now in place', the Pilgrimage began across the country on 18 June 1913.[46] Using various routes, the federations would enter London via one of six main points culminating with a meeting in Hyde Park on 26 July: nineteen speakers, each representing one federation would speak from nineteen platforms. Some women walked the entire route from as far afield as Cornwall or Aberdeenshire, others covered just a part but all were requested to wear a form of uniform – close to Harley's heart, in 1914 she herself would be in uniform, never to relinquish it. A compulsory raffia cockle-shell shaped badge, the traditional pilgrim symbol, to be pinned to the pilgrim's hat, was sold to all 'pilgrims' for 3d. Also compulsory was the red, white and green NUWSS sash – no doubt to differentiate them from the WSPU purple, white and green, photographic evidence indicates some women proudly wore armbands stating their home county. Photographs indicate pilgrims' pride in their cause; a similar pride, this time in her Unit, would be continuously replicated in photographs of women during the war.[47]

The 1913 Pilgrimage was the high point of many women's association with the suffrage movement. Poet Dora Sigerson recognised there is a strange 'joy where danger be'; some of the crowds the pilgrims encountered along the way were openly hostile despite the prominently displayed 'Non-Militant' banners.[48] Constitutional suffragists, with their much lower profile than the imprisoned, hunger-striking, not infrequently forcibly fed suffragettes, welcomed the publicity limelight which now finally shone upon them.[49]

Several pilgrims kept diaries recording how they were greeted at their stopping points. In Chelmsford (Essex), pilgrims were 'attacked by boys who threw green apples at their horses and wagonette … and destroyed the banner they were carrying.[50] This was not an isolated incident. The

*Daily News* commented that 'hooliganism was always worst in those places where anti-suffragists had held meetings the day preceding the arrival of the pilgrims'. Southampton member Harriet Blessey commented that it is 'difficult to feel a holy pilgrim when one is called a brazen hussy!'[51]

The Pilgrimage made a significant impact and reminded the public that most women were peacefully seeking the vote. The banner under which Millicent Fawcett addressed pilgrims at Hyde Park boldly proclaimed, 'Law-Abiding Suffragists'. Asquith even acceded to NUWSS leaders request for a meeting – the first with a suffrage deputation since November 1911. However, no change in government policy was forthcoming. Nevertheless, the pilgrimage had served its purpose, it had raised just under £9,000 (£945,000 today) and honed the organising skills of several key women who would play significant roles thirteen months later when war broke out. Reporting on the Pilgrimage, *The Times* (28 July) commented that 'the proceedings were orderly and devoid of any untoward incident'. Whether the organisers would have agreed that the 'proceedings were as much a demonstration against militancy as one in favour of women's suffrage' is a moot point.

In early 1914, building upon the Pilgrimage's successful foundations, Katherine Harley was involved in the formation of the Active Service League. By mid-August, the League had become a relief body, actively 'processing women who wished to assist in the war effort sending them onto organisations within which they could serve'.[52] Katherine offered her own personal message to the women of Shropshire, asking them to 'volunteer to take over men's jobs enabling them to go and fight. I ask this in the name of my brother [Sir John French] who so sorely needs the able-bodied men in the country.'[53] Before her departure for service with the first SWH Unit in France, the NUWSS leadership entrusted Katherine with the creation of the Active Service Girls' Cadet Corps which aimed to encourage girls to put their energy and enthusiasm to patriotic use and sought to mobilise young women and girls to work on the Home Front.

Outraged by the many wartime activities which seemingly linked women's desire for the vote with their war service and which articles in *Common Cause* made apparent, the October 1914 *Anti-Suffrage Review* published 'The Broken Truce' accusing the NUWSS of 'not respecting the political truce' tacitly agreed upon for the duration. The author (probably Mary

Ward) claimed that 'the NUWSS and *Common Cause* far from suspend[ing] ordinary political work' is 'doing a good deal of extraordinary political work, and with excellent result'.

The Anti-Suffrage League began accusing suffragists of 'cornering the market' in public service. Their *Review* petulantly claimed that 'they sew and knit comforts for soldiers but with such a perpetual running accompaniment of suffragist self-laudation that they might as well embroider the name of Mrs Pankhurst or Mrs Fawcett on every sock and muffler'.[54] Perhaps Mary Ward knew or suspected that some women enclosed notes saying 'Votes for Women' with their gifts or, when illustrating their war diaries and letters, wrote their slogan whenever women were shown performing tasks previously more commonly associated with males.[55]

Whatever the war of knitting needles or words fought by the NUWSS via *Common Cause*, many activists including Katherine Harley (who in 1916 was awarded the French Croix de Guerre avec Palme) and her young daughter who acted as a hospital orderly in France and Serbia, would soon be in the thick of the war, fighting disease, famine and horrific wounds. On 7 March 1917, Katherine was killed by Bulgarian shellfire at Monastir in Serbia. Remembered on an impressive memorial, one Serb soldier remarked 'To die for one's country … is fine; that we understand; but to die for another country that is superb – that is something beyond us.'[56] A number of suffragists died for their own or another's country.

## Marching to War:

Although women's processions are associated with the suffrage campaigns and as such concluded with the outbreak of war, Emmeline Pankhurst's involvement in these did not end on 4 August 1914. Ironically in the light of her bitter pre-war campaigns against the government, she would soon be working hand-in-hand with her former opponent, Lloyd George. On 24 June 1915, she had delivered a tub-thumping, well-reported speech on 'Women's Right To Serve'. George V asked Lloyd George 'whether it would be possible or advisable for you to make use of Mrs Pankhurst.'[57] Two days later, with a government subsidy of £2,000 (£212,000 today), plans were in hand for a procession to harness public opinion and endeavour to overturn Trades Union and industrialists' objections to employing significant numbers of women in munitions and other factories and trades.

Despite this handsome government subsidy, Emmeline quickly sought the upper hand; she presented this march as a WSPU initiative taking place in the face of what she termed the 'grave national danger' facing the country. The WSPU now requested women of all classes to participate in what was hoped would be the biggest demonstration of its kind ever seen. Banners, bands and women dressed in white were mustered. Women were also requested to wear not the WSPU's purple, white and green colours, but the red, white and blue of the Union flag. Emmeline's flair for rallying her troops remained undimmed, some 30,000 women signed up within a fortnight, eager to demonstrate that they too had a 'Right to Serve'. There is a striking similarity between images of women forming up to march in the pre-war suffrage processions and wartime ones when serving women marched in this and other rallies to promote their branch of war work. Banners which had demanded 'Votes for Women' now proclaimed women's desire to, for example, 'Drop Every Mortal Thing & Send Them Plenty of Munitions'.[58]

Providing a certain symmetry with that first Mud March of 1907, the 17 July weather was inclement, the 125 separate contingents of marchers arrived in driving rain and wind. Sensibly covering their white dresses with mackintoshes, they formed, in the words of the following Monday's *Daily Telegraph*, a 'stirring pageant of brown, grey and black'. Watched by an estimated 100,000 spectators and with ninety bands striking up the 'Marseillaise' followed by other anthems and patriotic songs, Emmeline led her troops from Whitehall across London's main thoroughfares and shopping streets (whose windows suffragettes had recently smashed) to the Embankment. To try to ensure that willing women-workers were immediately enlisted, 233 tables were set out where, shielded by tarpaulins, women could sign up for war work. Finally, under a now watery sun, Lloyd George, Minister of Munitions, received a deputation in Whitehall. Addressing the thousands of cheering women, he praised their organising capacities, of which he ruefully admitted he had previously 'been a victim', and stated his conviction that 'the women of the country can help achieve victory'. As well as being a march promoting women's Right to Serve, the procession was also a 'Pageant of the Allies'; to heartfelt applause a purple-and-black-clad barefoot young woman representing Gallant Little Belgium lead the way. The banner held aloft was not one of a suffrage society but a 'tattered flag of mourning'.[59]

Extensively reported in the newspapers, the pageantry and patriotism were widely praised. Apparent to reporters then as it should be to historians now, the main hallmarks of the suffrage processions and pageants had been expertly mobilised in support of a new cause. Superb organisational skills, representatives from all classes of society, spectacle and overwhelming enthusiasm (which even the driving rain could not dampen), had been harnessed to demonstrate women's eagerness to play their part in the war effort. However, although much has been made of the success, at least in terms of spectacle, of the Right to Serve March and of the War Work procession held exactly a year later, and attention drawn to how this rehabilitated Emmeline in the eyes of the state, the wartime demonstration in some ways 'marked the funeral of the Suffragette movement itself'.[60] Emmeline did not enjoy the press or the government's unanimous approval and in some circles at least, she continued to be treated with suspicion. Be that as it may, on this occasion, two of the country's most skilled demagogues had effectively worked side by side, although undoubtedly both with concealed ulterior motives. For Emmeline, this was the vote for middle-and upper-class women; for Lloyd George, this women's march was part of his campaign for the leadership of the Liberal Party and indeed the government itself.[61]

Forcefully underlining the chasm that had opened between mother and daughter, the same week Sylvia Pankhurst and Charlotte Despard's East London Federation (unlike Emmeline they remained committed to universal adult suffrage), had already demonstrated that millions of women were supporting the state at home. As the demonstration pointed out, their reward was (and largely remained) sweated wages.

## Suffragism Goes to War:

The self-confidence, fundraising and public-speaking skills acquired by suffrage campaigners – be they leaders or foot soldiers – and the lessons they learned, which went far beyond organising or participating in public spectacles, would be called upon and refined during the war. But now, rather than fighting the intransigence and duplicity of many politicians, activists were assisting their country in what many considered to be her hour of greatest peril. Some were determined that their wartime endeavours would contribute to women's post-war enfranchisement; others shelved their ardent desire for the vote 'for the duration'. Some saw War Work as the only patriotic course open to them, whilst for others, 'womanhood' and 'the vote' took, and would continue to take, precedence over nationality; they strove to remain loyal to and support the causes of peace and international suffragism.

The common denominator in all the women featured in this book is that they had earned their spurs in the tumultuous suffrage decades before the war. Women from all walks of life had entered the public arena. They had stood in the gutters, made 'spectacles' of themselves by marching in processions watched by thousands; they had been abused both verbally and physically by the police and at the behest of government ministers; they had been pelted with rotten food and heckled – and done their fair share of heckling – at public meetings. They had fundraised, created and published their own propaganda and many of them had learnt to work together and not get (too) bogged down in differences of opinion. They had formed pressure groups, some had broken and resisted the law and been imprisoned as common criminals. Above all they understood women's united strength and the strength that comes from sharing a common cause.

For many historians, the women's suffrage movement forms one significant chapter in women's history, and the First World War an equally significant yet separate one. However, women's experiences in the suffrage and indeed the anti-suffrage movements were fertile training grounds for all that they created and achieved during four and a half years of war. Far from the fight for the vote ending on 4 August 1914 and women's war work beginning shortly afterwards, all that had really changed for suffragists and suffragettes was the perceived 'enemy'. They merely adapted their skills to suit the war's realities for although a nation at war may be perceived as a male nation, this war could not have been won without the contributions of this 'monstrous regiment of [suffrage and anti-suffrage] women'.[62]

## Chapter Two

# Hunger for Change

Strangeways Prison, Manchester, is notorious for an April 1990 riot and for housing serial murderer Harold Shipman whilst awaiting trial. However, Strangeways has another, now overlooked, claim to fame. For a few nights in October 1905, it housed two women who raised women's demand for enfranchisement to a different level. Their actions utterly changed the face of the suffrage movement.

On 14 October, mill-worker Annie Kenney and law student Christabel Pankhurst were found guilty of assaulting the police and causing an obstruction during Liberal MP Sir Edward Grey's 13 October speech at the Free Trade Hall. Christabel was fined 10s (£56 today) or a jail sentence of one week; Annie 5s, or three days in prison. *Manchester Courier* (21 October) informed readers that whilst the magistrates were deliberating and considering their sentences, Christabel and Annie, alert to the oxygen of publicity, had put up a banner in the courtroom demanding 'Votes for Women'. Having refused to pay their fines, they were sent to prison, to the Second Division which necessitated wearing prison clothes and eating prison food.[1] Whether suffragettes were common criminals and thus considered Second (even Third) Division prisoners where conditions were much harsher, or political (First Division) ones, was never resolved. The Division depended on the whim of the court and, not infrequently, the woman's social class.[2] The many newspapers which featured the case were unaware that increasing suffrage militancy would become a running story for the next nine years.

Suffragists not sent to the First Division would in time resort to thirst, sleep, hunger strikes, sometimes all three at once, leading to the horrors of forcible feeding which many historians consider akin to rape or modern 'water-boarding'. Inflicted upon well over a thousand hunger-striking women and a significant number of men, forcible feeding has come to dominate the popular history of suffragism. Despite the Liberal government claiming that it was thereby ensuring that lives were not lost, even some (although far from all) anti–suffrage male doctors were outraged at its brutality, as an article in the medical journal *The Lancet* in August 1912 made plain.[3]

On release, most imprisoned suffragettes were greeted (preferably with suitable press coverage) at the prison gates. Fêted by non-militants and militants alike, those close to death were tenderly cared for by suffrage-supporting nurses and female doctors, banquets were held in the honour of those with sufficient strength. All were awarded medals 'For Valour'; additional clasps showed the number of imprisonments endured whilst hunger strikers had this additional commitment to the Cause engraved on their medals' reverse. These were worn with pride, none more so than by Mary Allen.

## Nina Boyle (1865–1943) and Mary Allen (1878–1964): Poachers turned gamekeepers.

On the outbreak of war, thousands of refugees flooded into England. In August 1914, approximately 260,000 refugees, mostly Belgian women and children, sought sanctuary in the UK; many were destitute, arriving with only the clothes they stood up in.[4] As soon as the 'refugee crisis' began, suffrage organisations set about offering assistance; a group of suffragists even visited the Belgian Embassy, where, as Edith Lyttleton remembered, Ambassador Count Charles-Maximilien de Lalaing, 'frightened by our vehemence' parted with £200 (£21,000 today) to enable the women to buy supplies for the refugees at Lyon's Corner House.[5]

Concerns for female and juvenile refugees extended far beyond helping to feed them. Pre-war, anxieties about the so-called 'White Slave Trade' (the trafficking of young girls around Europe to act as prostitutes) had flourished, leading to the formation of National Vigilance Associations (NVAs). Although the police were supposed to ensure incoming refugees' safety, fears quickly developed about young women falling prey to traffickers. Transport Committees were formed to protect potential victims; NVA members and the newly established uniformed Women's Emergency Corps began patrolling the main stations and reception centres, endeavouring to deter traffickers. By September 1914, these organisations were considered to have provided valuable, if ad hoc, services.

Committees need heads and, due to her connection with the pre-war Criminal Law Amendment Committee, the well-known, widely-respected philanthropist and animal welfare campaigner, Margaret Damer Dawson was quickly appointed head of the Chelsea Refugee Committee's Transport Committee.[6] Deeply concerned for refugees' safety, and assisted by other wealthy like-minded Chelsea residents, she began ferrying refugees from the London railway stations at which they had arrived. WSPU member Mary Allen, Margaret's future lover and second-in-command noted, 'it was whilst engaged in this work that the urgent need was forced upon her for a body of trained women in uniform whose *bona fides* might be unquestionable and recognisable at sight'.[7]

Suffragette Nina Boyle was thinking along similar lines. A veteran nursing auxiliary and journalist from the South Africa War, she had founded the Women's Enfranchisement League of Johannesburg; on returning to England in 1911, she became an active member and contributor to the militant Women's Freedom League (WFL)'s journal. By 1912, as well as being the WFL's political secretary, she was one of their main speakers and militant activists. In May 1913, she had been imprisoned for fourteen days for causing an 'obstruction'. As she explained in *Votes for Women* (23 May 1913), she and other female prisoners were conveyed to Holloway in a van containing men. They 'began to signal to us and make obscene gestures, from the sight of which it was impossible to hide'. She forced the Home Office to undertake investigations into her allegations. Inter alia, Charlotte Despard and Dr Elizabeth Knight swore on oath that, against government policy, women were often taken to prison in vans which also conveyed male convicts. Home Secretary Reginald McKenna must have found it galling to admit the veracity of the women's complaints which forced him into drawing up plans for new motorised vans or 'Black Marias'. These remained merely plans however, and following a subsequent arrest in July 1914, Boyle again complained. Her experiences convinced her that women should be policed not by men but by women.

When in August 1914 Nina learned that the Home Office was seeking about 20,000 recruits to work as police 'Specials', she suggested using women instead. She, like many other women, was deeply concerned about the possible revival of the loathed Contagious Diseases Act and of the likelihood of male officers policing laws that were 'almost exclusively concerned with matters in which women are involved to a greater extent than men'.[8] Initially mocked, she had nevertheless been organising volunteers and outlined her scheme in *The Vote* (21 August 1914) asking (not only suffrage) women to volunteer for duties hitherto 'performed by men constables' – and not exclusively the policing of women.

Although the London Commissioner of Police was at first reluctant to include women in his policing operations, this apparently 'had more to do with Nina's past suffrage activities' than with her actual scheme; when she and Margaret (not a former 'jailbird' nor even a prominent suffrage supporter) joined forces, the Commissioner became 'convinced that the past militancy of the suffrage movement was not now the issue [and] gave permission for the scheme to go ahead'.[9] However, they were given no training or advice beyond the titles of possible textbooks and the name of an ex-sergeant who could help with drill and ju-jitsu.[10] By September 1914, the Women Police Volunteers (WPV) were established, they had to declare willingness to go anywhere in the country and believed that they would be paid, full-time employees. Unlike many suffrage supporters, including Mary Allen, Nina was not prepared to fully suspend her suffrage activism 'for the Duration', thus Margaret became Commandant of the fledgling organisation albeit initially closely supported by Nina and many WFL members.

Mary held the distinction of being amongst the first women to be forcibly fed; she had undergone three spells in Holloway. Her suffrage past was in some ways more sensational than Nina's, her convictions as deep-rooted. A product of bourgeois Victorian/Edwardian England, when around 1908 Mary decided to commit herself to the suffrage campaign, her father's reaction was unequivocal, 'Either you give up this Suffragette nonsense absolutely and for good – or you leave this house!'[11] Despite being, as she put it, 'trained for no occupation', and showing the steely determination that hallmarked the rest of her life, she left the parental home (conveniently, although this was not anticipated, her father continued her allowance) and joined the WSPU. She was soon in Holloway. Her account of the grim conditions (including forcible feeding where 'one and a half pints of egg and milk were forced into my stomach through the nose in two minutes') alleviated by the camaraderie of fellow suffragette prisoners, is grimly compelling.[12] Nurse Pitman, a fellow militant sentenced with Mary in

November 1909, remembered the 'cries and moans of Miss Mary Allen ... who was fed twice a day'.[13]

Mary often broke prison rules: when sewing shirts, she embroidered 'Votes for Women on each tail in large letters.[14] Thirty years later, she calculated that there were over 100 shirts of 'unbleached calico' still used in Pentonville and Wormwood Scrubs bearing 'the regimental banners of a forgotten cause'.[15] Her organisational skills, eloquence and her involvement with training newer WSPU recruits were impressive. Deeply proud of her commitment, her medals and the fame (or notoriety) she enjoyed, pre-war she had proved adept at communicating with those in authority. On 13 August 1909, she had accompanied Labour MP Keir Hardie and Home Secretary Herbert Gladstone on a tour of inspection of the grim conditions in Holloway.

By August 1914, like countless others for whom the Cause had been everything, Mary with her now impressive array of skills, was amongst the 'changed women' for whom 'going home and resuming their former roles was not an option'.[16] Commenting a decade later on her and sister suffragettes' transformation from militants into policewomen, she acknowledged that 'their public [suffrage] work, including as it did haranguing crowds at all seasons, in all neighbourhoods, under the most unfavourable conditions, had taught them how to face with astonishing courage and resolution the most virulent forms of opposition – howling derision or personal violence'.[17]

Perhaps ironically, several key members of this early women's police force were former 'jailbirds' imprisoned for window-breaking, crimes against property and in one case, for trying to throw a petition into the king's carriage during a royal visit to Dundee in 1914. Now they would be working for, rather than against, the authorities. Although initially run on hardly more than a semi-voluntary basis, in 1916 the Service finally received a government grant although 'it never sufficed to free us from financial anxieties' and their leaders were constantly calling on fundraising skills acquired during the suffrage years.[18]

Mary herself was first 'called to arms' in November 1914.[19] With no powers of arrest (these could only be conferred on men), wearing a hard felt hat and a dark blue plainly cut (unfeminine) uniform with shoulder straps bearing the letters WPV in silver, Mary and colleague Ellen Harburn were sent to Grantham, a pre-war market town of some 20,000 souls whose population was increased by 18,000 with the establishment of a nearby Machine Gun Training Centre. This sudden influx made 'the streets and public places perilous'.[20] The women had been specifically requested to police the 'workless or unstable girls who hung about the outskirts of the camp. They were in no sense criminals; often they were simply carried away in an hysteria of patriotism and wished to give something – anything, even themselves – to the men who were so shortly going out to fight for England'.[21] Perhaps to the surprise of their would-be detractors, these two 'Pollies' proved eminently successful but, in a fashion that seems surprising in women who had previously been fighting male authority and promoting women's rights, their duties largely comprised keeping 'watch chiefly on disorderly women'.[22] Having been granted 'the right to enter any house, building or land within a six-mile radius of the Army Post Office,' to ensure that the thirteen-hour curfew imposed on 'women of loose character' was maintained, Mary and Ellen had aligned themselves with patriarchal authorities determined to control women's behaviour.[23] The poachers were now truly gamekeepers.

It was this aggressive policing of rather than supporting women (although in areas where there were undoubtedly hordes of drunken soldiers many women would have welcomed their presence) which led to a break with Nina Boyle. She had never envisaged a force that would place the interests of the military authorities over those of women and children, seemingly in total contradiction of wider suffrage aims. Her outrage was such that she succeeded in having the curfew (which she denounced as a 'slur upon *all* women'[24]) declared illegal and demanded not only Mary and Ellen's recall to London but also Margaret's resignation.[25] Nina had seriously miscalculated and when a meeting was called in London to try to resolve the situation, she found her views and supporters were out of touch with the majority of WPVs – even former militants.[26] Outmanoeuvred, in 1916, Nina went to Macedonia and Serbia and was awarded the Samaritan Order of Serbia for her war service. The renamed Women's Police Service (WPS) was now in the hands of a Council of Three: Margaret, Mary and former hunger-striker Isobel Goldingham. They moulded the organisation to their will.

Following their success in Grantham and Nina's demise, in May 1915, Mary and Ellen were sent to Hull. Here they experienced their first air raid and with the assistance of another suffrage woman, Dr Mary

Murdoch who was 'always the first to answer the call for help and could be seen at many air-raids', they did sterling work helping the injured and trying to exert control over those who were in an understandable state of panic.[27] Their achievements in Hull led to what became the WPS's most important role. Drawing some pay from the Treasury as well as from the local police forces in whose areas they worked, and unusually employed at the same rate as men, the WPS embarked upon their 'most formidable task': policing the munitions factories which by late 1915 were employing women in ever increasing numbers; Mary termed this, 'Active Service with a vengeance'.[28]

Whether it was Lloyd George who made the overtures for WPS to police the factories as stated in *Lady In Blue,* or Metropolitan Commissioner Sir Edward Henry's idea as claimed in *Pioneer Policewoman* matters little. In an April 1916 contract with the Ministry of Munitions, the WPS agreed to train and equip women on a six-month unpaid trial basis which placed the organisation in considerable financial embarrassment; only in January 1917 was a pay structure agreed. *The Times* (26 January 1917) reported 'three hundred women are wanted immediately'. The WPS was even tasked with recruiting women about to be released from Holloway. Rather than reminiscing with the inmates about her own sojourns in Holloway, Mary told them that by sitting in cells 'eating food that other people had paid for' they were showing themselves to be 'enemies of their own country'. The ploy worked and many ex-convicts applied for jobs – Mary smugly feels that had she and Margaret been given longer for this recruitment drive, 'we could have got many more'.[29]

Munitions police work was arduous and frequently dangerous with the constant risk of explosions. There was also the need for significant tact and, at times, a hard heart. One of the WPS's duties was to ensure that no potentially flammable material was carried on site, all workers were searched prior to entering the danger sheds. Anyone even inadvertently contravening the rule was instantly dismissed. There were also trouble-spreaders as WPS Gabrielle West reported 'Last night [16 July 1917] as I was preparing to go home ... I found a girl who was last week discharged from the factory hanging round the gates. She refused to go away and said she was sure the factory was going to be blown up etc.' Having repeated the information to the next shift, 'none of them would go to back to work but stayed outside in a wild state of excitement'. The girl was later 'certified insane and sent to an asylum'.[30]

Explosions and air-raids were a constant source of danger and understandable fear. The 4 October 1918 *Police Chronicle* would not have made reassuring reading: 'There is no air-raid shelter available for the Policewomen and their station is the simplest kind of wooden structure which is fitted with a roof.' During one raid, 'one could distinguish the splinters of shells and the shrapnel dropping on the roofs of the buildings while every now and then the air is torn by a terrific explosion of an enemy bomb'. Keen to promote the sterling work and character of the WPS, the report goes on to say that far from cowering with fear, 'the WPS were discovered in their little hut calmly drinking tea and chatting among themselves', a subsequent report noted how the women's calm bravery was 'infectious'. Self-publicist Mary was, understandably, keen to include such ardent praise for the WPS in her autobiographies.

In November 1918 with well over 1,000 trained policewomen working either alongside or independently of male colleagues, Mary and the higher echelons of the WPS anticipated that the force, in recognition of their (amply documented) loyal assistance since the outbreak of war, would be rewarded with policewomen being integrated into the peacetime service. Their hopes were soon dashed. Nevil Macready had replaced their champion, Sir Edward Henry, as Metropolitan Commissioner of Police. Mary's and other WPS leaders' suffragette past came back to haunt them. Although the Metropolitan Police's website explains that Macready, cognisant of the WPS's 'obtrusive policing of prostitutes, harassing the women without acting against their clients', refused to adopt them as Metropolitan Police aides, it is probable that part of the reason behind his refusal was antipathy towards their suffragism.[31] Using language resembling that used in the anti-suffrage press against the pre-war suffrage women, he explained, 'The main point was to eliminate any woman of extreme views – the vinegary spinster or blighted middle-aged fanatic'.[32] A further nail in their coffin was that Macready, who in twenty-first century terminology would be called homophobic, considered Margaret and Mary to be 'sexual inverts' and therefore unsuitable to head an authority which properly belonged to men.

The two wartime Chiefs went on the offensive. In February 1920, a Home Office Inquiry was established to consider the 'Employment of Women on

Police Duties'. It was apparent that this was a hopeless task and the strains of defending the Service to which many women had given their all proved too much for Margaret. Mary believed that Margaret's death in May 1920 aged 46, of valvular heart disease and syncope, was 'hastened by her bitter disappointment at the treatment she received after the war'.[33] Like so many women, the WPS Commandant and Deputy Commandant who in July 1919 were fêted at a Buckingham Palace Garden Party and praised by the Prince of Wales for their 'four years service', had no place in the brave new post-war England. Having stood unsuccessfully as a Liberal parliamentary candidate, with a manifesto that included the 'recognition of women police as an essential public service', not to mention the 'extension of the women's franchise', Mary eventually forged an international career for herself advising foreign governments on how to implement a women's police force.[34]

Whilst Mary Allen was fighting for the survival of the WPS, her erstwhile colleague and subsequent opponent Nina Boyle was involved in a battle closer to her suffrage roots. She attempted to stand as a WFL candidate in the March 1918 Keighley by-election, the first woman nominated as a parliamentary candidate. However, according to the Returning Officer and an election petition judge 'she could not be nominated because, in common law, if a thing had not been it could not be until a statute was passed enabling it to be'.[35] This was soon overturned and she was initially told that she could stand. However, a technical error subsequently detected in her papers prevented her from standing. Like many post-war suffragists, Nina became involved with the 'Save the Children Fund'. With the oppression of women still close to her heart, she became a champion of women's rights in South Africa, Ceylon, Mauritius and China. Her 1927 novel *The Rights of Mallaroche*, made the *Times Literary Supplement* reviewer 'smile at the feminism which Miss Boyle has kept hot from her suffragette days'.[36] In his obituary, the MP F. W. Pethwick-Lawrence praised 'her dazzling wit, her splendid comradeship and the vigorous part she played in all activities that came her way'.

Mary Allen OBE died in December 1964, her reputation tarnished by her support for Franco, Hitler and fascism. Whatever her policies in the tormented post-war years, Mary had fought doggedly for two causes in which she passionately believed: female enfranchisement and a Women's Police Service. It would no doubt give her great satisfaction to know that in April 2017, Cressida Dick CBE was appointed head of the Metropolitan Police.[37] Women's contribution to policing, the value of which the suffragette founders of the wartime WPS underlined, has finally proved the lie of the words spoken in 1922 by the Liberal Home Secretary Edward Shortt, 'their work was not police work, no matter how noble'.

### Alice Wheeldon (1866–1919) 'kind, zealous, energetic'.

Whilst Mary Allen's WPS were enthusiastically policing (female) munitions workers, MI5 was involved in undercover factory surveillance activities. Following explosions in munitions factories, Minister of Munitions Lloyd George began to fear that at least some of these were caused not by poor design and cost cutting but by sabotage. On 19 February 1916, he created the Ministry of Munitions Labour Intelligence Division (MMLI), subsequently renamed Parliamentary Military Security Department, No.2 (P.M.S.2).[38] Methods included using agents, disguised as conscientious objectors on the run from the authorities, to make contact with 'conchies' and left-wing activists and report back any subversive activities. Disbanded in April 1917, P.M.S.2 destroyed the reputation of suffragette Socialist Labour Party and No-Conscription Fellowship (NCF) member, Alice Wheeldon, the proprietor of a second-hand clothes shop in Peartree Road, Derby.

Pre-war, Alice and her adult daughters had joined Derby's very active WSPU, both Christabel and Emmeline Pankhurst visited the town on several occasions.[39] Although committed to suffragism, it is unlikely that Alice was involved in law-breaking activities as there is no pre-war police record. She sold the WSPU's *The Suffragist*, and Sylvia Pankhurst subsequently remembered her as 'the kind of zealous, energetic volunteer worker who is the backbone of any movement'.[40] In June 1914, when the suffragette arson campaign was at its height, a devastating fire occurred at Breadsall Church, Derbyshire. Never conclusively proved, some evidence pointed to suffragette action.[41] Although there was no mention of the Wheeldons at the time, subsequent hearsay pointed a finger of blame at them. This would prove inflammatory.

When war broke out, the Wheeldons did not obey Emmeline Pankhurst's command to throw their weight behind the war effort and use every means within their power to encourage men to enlist. Very much the opposite. They became deeply involved with the NCF and the Socialist Labour

Party. Alice's schoolteacher daughter Harriet (Hettie) was engaged to Arthur MacManus, a Socialist Labour Party activist and member of the Clyde Workers' Committee with probable connections with the anarcho-syndicalist Industrial Workers of the World as well as with the NCF.[42] Alice's other daughter, WSPU member Winnie, and her chemist husband Alf Mason, lived in Southampton, she was a schoolteacher, his position as a laboratory assistant at Hartley University College provided access to various poisons including the deadly curare.

Many feminist pacifists and former suffragists were active within the NCF, using tactics of their suffragist past to non-violent ends in their struggle against conscription. If in the past the prison miseries of suffrage supporters had been carefully documented, now suffragist/pacifists attended the trials and kept records of men imprisoned for their conscientious beliefs.[43] Hettie was Secretary of the Derby NCF, keeping records pertaining to Derby's COs – although she felt enthusiasm for the cause was waning. Crucially for the case that would be constructed against the Wheeldons, the police intercepted their letters detailing the conchies' prison treatment.

A big munitions area, a producer of Ambulance Trains and aero-engines, Derby had also become the centre of clandestine opposition to the war. The anti-monarchist, pro-Labour Wheeldon home was, according to 3 January 1920 *Workers Dreadnought*, a 'haven for anyone opposed to the war'. *Derby Mercury* (9 March 1917) reported that it 'was common knowledge to most people' that Alice's Peartree Road home/shop acted as temporary sanctuary to men on the run from the police for resisting conscription and also for those endeavouring to escape to the USA. The Wheeldons also tried to alleviate the significant financial and emotional sufferings inflicted by a vindictive government not only on COs but also on their wives. They were very far from alone but the 'spotlight of history fell on them partly because they had familial and friendship links with agitators in the factories and therefore with industrial militancy'.[44]

Increasingly fearful of 'industrial militancy', Ministry of Munitions informers were 'pre-occupied with preventing three strategic dangers: an alliance between skilled and unskilled workers; the creation of a national rank and file movement, and a link between industrial unrest in essential industries and the NCF.'[45] All seemed to present very real threats and, unsurprisingly, factory owners welcomed the army of informers and spies that MI5 so generously offered to send. They were supposedly informing on foreign and home-grown agitators and saboteurs. Contrary to many of the sycophantic press reports about the female 'munitionettes' there was, as WPS (inter alia) Gabrielle West and Mary Allen make plain, significant female unrest in the factories relating to pay and conditions. Government agents who either made no attempt or were unable to understand the causes behind the industrial unrest which was now hindering the war effort, accused women of involvement in subversive activities.

Perhaps doubly damning the Wheeldons, Ministry of Munitions spies were also carrying out surveillance on suffrage supporters who had expressed anti-war sentiments and known pacifists, of which despite the Pankhursts' best efforts, there were considerable numbers. The government or at least their agents' reasoning seemed to be that involvement with one type of protest meant involvement with all others.[46]

In December 1916, one 'Alex Gordon' (Francis Vivian) arrived at Peartree Road. His background in the British Socialist Party led to Alice taking his credentials, including his cover story of being a conchie on the run, at face value. But, despite being a former radical socialist of dubious character, he was now in the employ of the intelligence services; his task: infiltrate organisations deemed subversive. He was offered the Wheeldons' safe house on 27 December 1916; he introduced them to one 'Comrade Bert', in reality Herbert Booth, his handler.

Alice and her daughter Winnie exchanged constant coded (a well-established suffrage ploy) letters in which they gave vent to their anti-war/anti-government/anti-monarchist sentiments. Their code was based around the statement, 'We will hang Lloyd George from a sour apple tree'. Gordon would later claim that he had heard Alice comment that George V would be the last English monarch. Alice's coded request to Winnie that her husband send four phials of the poison curare was the nail in their coffin. It was assumed that the intended victim was not, as the Wheeldons subsequently claimed, the dogs guarding the camp where COs were held but the Prime Minister, Lloyd George. Suffragettes' attacks on Lloyd George, or at least his property, were still fresh in the government's mind. On 20 February 1913, *The Times* had reported 'An attempt was made yesterday morning to blow up a house which is being built for Mr Lloyd George near Walton Heath Golf Links'. Speaking in Cardiff, Emmeline Pankhurst had claimed full responsibility for the explosion which had caused about £500 (£52,500 today) worth of damage; to her chagrin, another had failed to ignite. Her justification for this and similar actions was the government's hounding of suffragettes and failure to adhere to their request for Votes for Women.

It now seemed as though known suffragettes were hatching a plot in 'red Derby' to poison the King's First Minister. Herbert Booth reported that Alice had said to him that she hoped 'the bugger, [Lloyd George] would soon be dead' and directly linked the suffragettes with the plot.[47] The parcel containing the phials was intercepted, Alice and Hettie were arrested in Derby and the Masons in Southampton. Charged under the Offences Against the Person Act (1861) with 'conspiring to assassinate the prime minister, David Lloyd George, together with the prominent Labour Party war supporter Arthur Henderson and other unspecified persons, by firing poisoned darts' tipped with curare at them whilst they played golf.'[48] Nowadays, the case seems far-fetched but in the volatile wartime atmosphere with suffragette militancy still so recent, it seemed (just) believable that two working-class Socialist suffragettes were attempting to strike at the very heart of government.

When arraigned, Alice Wheeldon agreed to having received the poison sent by her son-in-law but vehemently denied plotting to kill Lloyd George. Briefly held in custody in Derby then transferred to Aylesbury Prison, the three Wheeldon women and Alf Mason were sent to trial at the London Royal Courts of Justice thereby guaranteeing maximum publicity. Rather ineptly defended by a Persian lawyer, Dr Riza, against whom a xenophobic press unleashed all its venom, the Crown's case was led by none other than the committed anti-suffragist Attorney General, F. E. Smith. Playing on the Wheeldon women's political affiliations and beliefs, he had a field day. Fearful that Alex Gordon's evidence might not stand up to scrutiny, he was carefully spirited away leaving Herbert Booth as key witness for the prosecution. Basil Thomson, Assistant Commissioner of the Metropolitan Police, admitted unease about the case and the disappearance of Gordon, 'I had an uneasy feeling that he might have acted as an agent provocateur'.[49] This unease did not stretch to calling a halt to the trial and the skilled Smith, at the peak of his powers and barely hiding his antipathy towards suffragism and pacifism, destroyed the meagre defence that Riza put up on his clients' behalf.

With the defendants presented to the undoubtedly biased, all-male jury as 'a gang of desperate persons poisoned by revolutionary doctrines and possessed of complete and unreasonable contempt for their country', a 'Guilty' verdict was inevitable.[50] Alice would have done nothing to endear herself to either jury or spectators by admitting under 'cross-examination that she hated Lloyd George and had referred to him and Henderson as "buggers"'[51] – much stronger terminology, especially when used by a woman, in 1917 than in 2017. On 10 March, Alice Wheeldon, Alfred and Winifred Mason were sentenced to ten, seven and five years' penal servitude. Hettie was acquitted but nevertheless lost her job as a teacher – she not being considered a fit person to shape young minds. Although she was eventually moved to Holloway, Alice began her sentence in Aylesbury where the even more vehemently anti-British Constance Markievicz was also imprisoned. Constance remembered meeting Alice who told her that she 'had never tried to kill Lloyd George'.[52] A further accusation levelled against Alice was of being a Sinn Féin supporter through her involvement with helping 'conchies' to escape to Ireland.

Following the example of the pre-war militant suffragettes, Alice embarked on hunger strikes although she was spared the torture of forcible feeding. In December 1918, with the war over, her health deteriorating, and following an intervention by Lloyd George, Alice was released on licence (not pardoned). With suffrage experience still fresh in his mind, he may have 'thought she should on no account be allowed to die in prison.... Her early release was again proof of the care the government took to avoid creating martyrs.'[53]

In Derby Alice met with significant hostility. Her modest business collapsed and she was reduced to eking out a living by growing tomatoes in the front room of 907 London Road. As did millions who contracted the disease, she died of influenza in February 1919, at the age of 53. Buried in a simple ceremony, 'devoid of Christian content' as befitted her atheist principles, her son William held the Red Flag over her coffin as it was lowered into the ground.[54] With the ending of the war and the cooling of emotions, few people in Derby truly believed her guilty of plotting to kill Lloyd George, seeing her instead as the victim of a vindictive Attorney General, determined to secure a conviction, even on the flimsiest of evidence, against a woman who stood for everything he loathed: pacifism, socialism and suffragism. Writing nine years later, in a shamelessly partial (and in places untruthful) account,

Smith said that the case 'served to emphasise the unanimity of the nation to prosecute the war with the utmost vigour to its successful conclusion'.[55]

Derby tradition maintains that Alice's ghost walks the tunnels under the Guildhall where she was briefly imprisoned before her trial. Should her descendants prove successful in their campaign to have the flawed verdict overturned, perhaps WSPU and ILP member, pacifist, outspoken feminist socialist Alice Wheeldon will, a century after her defamation, finally rest in peace in her unmarked grave in Derby's Nottingham Road cemetery.

## Constance Markievicz (1868–1927) 'The People's Countess'.

In his poem 'In Memory of Eva Gore-Both and Con Markievicz', Irish poet W. B. Yeats remembers the two sisters as, 'Two girls in silk kimonos, both / Beautiful'. He adds that whilst one (Eva) is 'a gazelle / the other, the older is condemned to death / Pardoned, drags out lonely years / Conspiring among the ignorant'. This not altogether flattering description of the 'older' sister relates to Constance, the daughter of Anglo-Irish landed gentry.

There was nothing in either sister's early years that suggested that they would throw in their lot with the suffrage movement. Born to privilege and home-educated by governesses at the family's Lissadell estate, County Sligo, they spent their adolescent years in typical country pursuits, hunting, driving and, in Constance's case, becoming an excellent markswoman. Many years later, when giving fashion advice, she commented, 'dress suitably in short skirts and strong boots. Leave your jewels in the bank and buy a revolver'.[56] Advice she would follow. Again, in manner typical of their class, the sisters were involved with philanthropic 'good works', visiting the poor and needy – of which there were plenty in County Sligo. Constance's commitment to the poor would in due course earn her the moniker 'The People's Countess'.

Somewhat ironically in terms of her later career and the Queen's views on 'this mad wicked folly of women's rights', the beautiful 19-year-old Constance was, as befitted a wealthy upper-class young woman, presented at Court in 1887. However, a rebellious streak was developing. To her family's disapproval, she enrolled at the Slade School of Art in 1893, a school proud of its tradition of gender equality and where several suffrage women studied. She had already started to show an 'impulsive interest' in London's down-and-outs, 'bringing home beggars and derelicts of both sexes for a meal, a warm-up, some clothes'.[57] Her interest in society's flotsam and jetsam mirrors that of Sylvia Pankhurst, Charlotte Despard and her own sister Eva who left Ireland and began carving a name for herself working amongst the working-class in Manchester. Eva was committed to both women's suffrage and was also co-secretary of the Manchester and Salford Women's Trade Council. (It was thanks to Eva, who was by 1900 a NUWSS member, that Christabel Pankhurst joined the North of England Society for Women's Suffrage's Executive Committee where she honed her debating skills.[58])

Constance too was interested in women's suffrage; in 1896, she presided over a meeting of the Sligo Women's Suffrage Society. Moving to Paris to further her studies and, eager to 'mine life's dreamy, seamy side', Constance met and married a Polish widower six years her junior, Count Casimir Dunin-Markievicz, the scion of Ukrainian landowners.[59] Returning to Ireland, the marriage was far from happy.

Constance's now growing interest in Irish Nationalism ran in parallel with her commitment to women's suffrage. In 1908, when visiting Eva in Manchester, she spurned Eva's constitutionalist NUWSS and joined the militant WSPU nailing her colours to their purple, white and green mast. In 1908 alongside other WSPU members, she disrupted Winston Churchill's by-election campaign by driving a four-in-hand plastered with slogans about barmaids' employment rights, a cause Eva had been championing. By 1913, Constance had Prime Minister Asquith in her sights; during his visit to Dublin, she grabbed a megaphone to ensure that he was not deaf to Irish women's demands for the Vote. She was behind the showering of both Asquith and Irish parliamentary leader John Redmond, with confetti demanding 'Votes for Women' as they drove through Dublin.

This was not the first anti-British protest she had staged. In 1911, she was arrested during George V's visit to Ireland, not on this occasion for suffrage activities but for protesting against the British monarchy. An executive member of both Sinn Féin and Inghinidhe na hÉireann, she was involved with training and mobilising the Irish Citizen Army and the Fianna.[60] Irish nationalism, suffragism and Trade Unionism (including the Irish Women Workers Union) were marching in step with her concern for the poorest of Ireland's very poor, Dublin workers' standard of living was thought to be the lowest in Europe.

When war was declared and so many suffragists threw themselves into supporting the war effort (although not Eva Gore-Booth who, with her friend Esther Roper, became a pacifist), Constance's commitment to Irish Nationalism took centre stage. This led her into the direct conflict with the British Government which defined the remainder of her life. The question of Irish involvement in Britain's War was a vexed one for many Irishmen and women, so much so that the government never dared introduce conscription. A co-founder of the Irish Neutrality League, Constance believed that the 200,000 Irishmen who had volunteered were 'deluded fools', agreeing instead with those who, in James Connolly's words, felt that, 'should a German Army land in Ireland tomorrow, we would be justified in joining it'.[61] Like Connolly and countless others she saw the British Empire as a Brigand Empire, and the way forward was that of Major John McBride and Sir Roger Casement. Her Dublin home, Surrey House, with its clandestine printing press working overtime to churn out anti-government propaganda and pro-German manifestos, became a 'haunt of rebels'. Soon under police surveillance, Constance took to using aliases and disguises and, with the so-called Citizen Army, took part in manoeuvers in anticipation of the promised German Expeditionary Force landing to crush the British garrisons stationed on Irish soil. With Connolly openly stating, 'we may yet see the day that the trenches will be safer for these [English] gentry than any part of Dublin', rebellion was in the air;[62] Markievicz was ecstatic, 'Our heart's desire was granted to us,' she wrote later, 'and we counted ourselves lucky'.[63]

On 25 April 1916, Staff Lieutenant Markievicz had the great honour (particularly for a woman) of being placed second-in-command of a troop of Irish Citizen Army combatants at St Stephen's Green. In no way due to her gender, Constance's battalion was outmanoeuvred by the British troops sent in to quell the rebellion. After a week of bitter fighting, several Dublin streets were reduced to rubble. By a strange coincidence, and one that reminds us that despite having tried to cast her antecedents behind her, she was a member of the Anglo-Irish gentry, a kinsman, 'Captain de Courcy Wheeler, Kings Royal Rifle Corps, accepted Staff Lieutenant Markievicz's surrender' – and her Mauser which she first kissed.[64] Marched into captivity, the question on everyone's mind was: would the ringleaders be hanged (the civilian penalty for treason), or shot (the military one)?

Subject to solitary confinement and unaware of her own fate as she had not yet been brought to trial, all Constance could do was listen to the shots that rang out as former friends and colleagues, including James Connolly, were hastily executed. As suffragist Esther Roper presciently wrote, 'The executions at Kilmainham and Pentonville were the worst days' work ever done by England to Ireland.'[65] In her poem *Easter Week*, Constance's pacifist suffragist sister Eva wrote of her 'Grief for the noble dead / Of one who did not share their strife / And mourned that any blood was shed'. Would Constance's blood too be shed?

On 4 May 1916, court-martialled for 'causing disaffection among the civilian population of His Majesty', Constance was found guilty and sentenced to death. Perhaps aware of the outrage caused by the Germans' execution of Nurse Edith Cavell some five months earlier, the flames of which the British authorities had enthusiastically fanned, this was commuted to penal servitude for life 'solely and simply on account of her sex'.[66] Rather than being held in Dublin, Constance was transferred to Aylesbury Prison, which had so recently incarcerated suffragettes, including those on hunger strike, and would soon house WSPU member Alice Wheeldon.

Held as a common criminal as opposed to a political prisoner and denied the privileges allowed to male political prisoners, some felt Constance was being punished for being a woman who had broken the bonds of womanly behaviour. The tedium of her life was alleviated by pacifist Eva's visits to whom Constance wrote, 'Dearest old Darling, ... I knew all the time you'd try and see me, even though I'd been fighting and you hate it all and think killing so wrong...', as well as official prison visitors.[67] One, Lady Constance Battersea, a key figure in Jewish Feminism was herself associated with suffrage, feminism, prison reform and alleviating poverty.[68] Another was penal reformist Adeline, Duchess of Bedford who, like both Constances, was closely involved with philanthropic work. However, suffragettes had identified Adeline as a 'penal repression collaborator' as she intervened in the matter of hunger-striking suffragettes in prisons between 1908 and 1914. She visited these and put it to them that they were committing sin in so risking their lives ... They particularly resented her public glossing of the suffering inflicted by forcible feeding in the prisons.[69]

Imprisonment did not damp Constance's Irish nationalism, she refused to go to the Prison Chapel to pray for an Allied victory. Released in June 1917 as part of the government's attempt at 'reconciliation', she received a tumultuous welcome in Dublin – and began to re-organise the Volunteers in a new bid for Irish liberation, she came fifth in the ballot of leadership of Sinn Féin.[70] When in March 1918 the British Army faced the very real prospect of defeat on the Western Front, Edward Shortt, who would be so disparaging about women's police work, was tasked with trying to introduce conscription in Ireland. Having assiduously fanned the flames of resistance 'with speeches hurled like grenades', Constance was rearrested and sent to Holloway.[71]

A strange honour awaited her. In the December 1918 election, Constance Markievicz stood for the St Patrick Division of Dublin. The only winner amongst the nineteen female candidates across the United Kingdom, she was unable to attend the opening of that newly convened House which included members elected by the 8 million newly enfranchised women. Even had she not been incarcerated, she, like all other Sinn Féiners would have refused to take her seat – although 'a clothes peg with her name mutely awaited her arrival'.[72] Remembering lessons of the suffragette days, she and ninety-two other prisoners went on hunger strike, four weeks later she was released.

After a third prison term, disillusioned by the bitter divisiveness of Ireland's internal politics, 'the People's Countess' dedicated the remainder of her life and her ever diminishing financial means to the poor who still swarmed in every back street in Dublin. In June 1927, she was hospitalised and, according to her wishes, was nursed in a public ward, dying on 15 July. Having lain in state in the Rotunda Cinema – the British Government having refused her mortal remains the honour of lying in the Mansion House, Dublin's poor patiently queued to pay their last respects. Wary of her potential continuing hold over Irish nationalists, soldiers with machine guns 'stood by to prevent a volley of honour being fired over her grave'.[73] The Last Post having sounded, Eamon de Valera gave the eulogy 'the friend of the toiler, the lover of the poor … is gone'.

Although Constance's suffragism was eventually subsumed in the bitter struggle for Irish independence and a war waged against what she saw as an oppressive government, she, like so many suffragists, was 'clothed with physical courage as with a garment'.[74]

*Chapter Three*

# 'Deeds not Words'

## 'Black Friday' 18 November 1910.

In the twenty-first century, 'Black Friday' conjures up images of desperate shoppers exchanging blows and wrestling each other to the ground in their attempts to acquire the latest consumer desirables. Although the first 'Black Friday' on 18 November 1910 ended in intense fighting, here the similarities end.

In June 1910, a Conciliation Bill, enfranchising women householders and those occupying premises with a rateable value of £10 per annum, was presented in Parliament. Although far from offering universal female enfranchisement, both the NUWSS and WSPU believed this was a step in the right direction. The WSPU called a militancy truce whilst the Bill progressed through the House. Having passed its second reading with a majority of 110, partial female enfranchisement seemed imminent. However, on 23 July, Asquith refused to grant the facilities which would have allowed the Bill to pass into law. Facing a constitutional crisis, in November he announced Parliament would soon be dissolved.

Outraged by Asquith's perceived treachery, on 10 November Emmeline Pankhurst announced to massed crowds of suffragettes at London's Royal Albert Hall that a deputation of WSPU members would seek a meeting with Asquith on 18 November to request the Conciliation Bill's passage. To a Hall 'filled with angry suffragettes' and playing the audience in the manner that was particularly her own (which she eventually placed at the service of the government), she vowed, 'If the Bill is killed by the Government … there is an end to the truce.'[1] Needing to obey 'public order' laws, small groups not exceeding twelve women would attempt to enter Parliament's male-only hallowed space and, if the first group led by Emmeline accompanied by hand-picked, high-profile minions, was denied entry, then the baton would pass to the second group and so on. To make sure that Honourable Members could not ignore the women's presence, chants would increase in volume as their numbers swelled.

Women clamoured to accompany Emmeline as she attempted to beard Asquith in his hallowed den. Those selected included 34-year-old Princess Sophia Duleep Singh and the elderly Dr Elizabeth Garrett Anderson (Millicent Fawcett's sister), England's first female doctor and mayor, accompanied by her doctor daughter, Louisa, whose participation put her own medical career on the line; she anticipated using her skills before the day ended. Hertha Ayrton, the first woman to be accepted into the Institute of Electrical Engineers and one of only two women to receive the Hughes Medal for Science, was also amongst the vanguard.

Emmeline had dressed for a photogenic arrest in a full-length fur coat and a black hat sporting 'tall black feathers'.[2] To loud cheers and intoning their battle-song, 'March of the Women', the first delegation left Caxton Hall accompanied by hundreds of others who would follow them into battle. They set out into the grey November morning to walk to Parliament Square; to Lady Rhondda this route became women's 'via dolorosa'.[3] Rumours of increased police presence swirled around, apparently England's youngest ever Home Secretary, Winston Churchill, was determined to teach the women a lesson – but not one involving arrests and potential martyrdom. According to several sources, policemen had been specially imported from the East End where they were more used to handling 'roughs' than suffragette ladies.[4] Neither side envisaged the scale of the impending confrontation.

A phalanx of police including mounted ones awaited this first delegation composed of England's most illustrious women; they would be followed in waves by some 300 suffragettes. Although many marchers were familiar with police tactics, they were ill-prepared for the level of the police presence and ensuing brutality. Ordered by Churchill to avoid being provoked into making arrests, the police beat, kicked, and sexually assaulted the petitioners. Women had their breasts gripped and twisted ('often done in the most public way so as to inflict maximum humiliation' there was a belief that such treatment could lead to breast cancer), women's skirts were lifted, knees thrust between their legs and their faces rubbed against railings – in full view of the Mother of Parliaments.[5] The assault lasted some six hours by which time 115 women and four men had been arrested, although Churchill subsequently ordered their release without charge as 'no public advantage would be gained by proceeding with the prosecution'.[6] The most iconic image of that grim

November day remains that of middle-aged Ada Wright on the front page of the next day's *Daily Mirror*. The photograph of her tiny cowering figure prostrate on the ground, shielding her face from a policeman whose foot is raised close to her coat, shocked readers. She subsequently claimed the government seized copies of the newspaper and demanded the negative to be destroyed.[7] Made of stern stuff, Ada remained militant throughout the campaign; she was a pallbearer at Emmeline's funeral. Although Churchill may have prevented women being imprisoned, he could not prevent two of them (Emmeline's sister, Mary Clarke, and war commander Sir Douglas Haig's kinswoman Cecilia) dying almost certainly from their injuries.[8]

Suffrage-supporting journalist H. N. Brailsford and Dr Flora Murray collected testimony from numerous women – all stressed police brutality and twenty-nine some form of sexual assault. *The Treatment of Women Deputations by the Metropolitan Police* with its plea for a public enquiry was forwarded to the Home Office. This make grim reading.[9] Seeking maximum damage limitation, Churchill called these testimonies, 'A copious fountain of mendacity'.[10] Metropolitan Police Commissioner Edward Hunt claimed the allegations were without foundation. Like the beleaguered Home Secretary, he appeared eager to brush the whole incident under the carpet. No public enquiry ensued. For many early twentieth century Edwardians, of both genders, by forsaking their god-ordained private/domestic space and entering the male 'public one' and transgressing gender boundaries, suffragists deserved such treatment. Little could anyone have guessed that within four years, Louisa and her colleague Flora Murray would enter one of the most hallowed of male public spaces, a Military Hospital, this time not as trespassers but as invited medical practitioners.

## Louisa Garrett Anderson (1873–1943) and Flora Murray (1869–1923) 'Doing a Superior Job'.

Reporting on the infamous events of 'Black Friday', *Votes for Women* noted Dr Louisa Garrett Anderson's 'pale, calm and quiet', presence. Inside, she felt less 'calm'. As surgeon at the New Hospital for Women, her presence might jeopardise her position. She informed the Chairman of the New Hospital Committee that, 'after serious consideration,' she had decided 'to go on the deputation to the Prime Minister'; having apologised for being unable to arrange hospital cover, she acknowledged the possibility of her arrest.[11] Her standing as a doctor was at stake, a prison sentence might lead to her being 'struck off'. She may have been the 'woman doctor' mentioned in *The Times* 19 November report whom the magistrate advised to apologise for her 'trivial assault' on a police officer and get the charge withdrawn. A suffrage supporter for over seven years, originally of her aunt Millicent's NUWSS and since 1907 the WSPU, she had persuaded her mother Elizabeth to 'defect' to the militants. An active committee member, she juggled being a surgeon and WSPU speaker. Through the WSPU, she had become close friends with Dr Flora Murray who, undeterred by the criticisms she attracted, was an outspoken critic of forcible feeding, airing her views in the learned and popular press. This friendship and professional collaboration would eventually benefit thousands of wounded British and Allied servicemen.

Neither imprisoned nor struck off the medical register, Louisa felt further militancy was required. Although she had voiced uncertainty about the wisdom of the campaign, in March 1912 she was sentenced to six weeks in prison with hard labour for throwing a stone through the window of a Knightsbridge residence, a sentence 'greeted with applause'.[12] Her prison term increased her commitment to the suffrage cause and her understanding of the harshness of her fellow prisoners' lives. She explained to her mother,

> The vast proportion … are here for petty theft connected with street walking! Charged by the men who have used them! No outside evidence being given. It is too hideously mean, isn't it? In itself ample reason for being a suffragist.[13]

From Holloway, she informed the Home Secretary, 'I had nothing to gain by the act for which I am now in prison: on the contrary, it involved considerable loss socially and probably great loss professionally. All this I realised before I committed it.'[14] Released two weeks early, she drew public attention to how prison treatment differed according to social class, whilst 'the Home Office thought I might like to spend Easter with my family', working-class women remained behind bars.[15] She rightly believed that her brother Alan (who did not share the distaff side of his family's beliefs) had a hand in her release. Maintaining her commitment to suffragism through both words and deeds, she protested about forcible feeding in the complicit

*British Medical Journal.*[16] With Flora Murray she helped run the Notting Hill nursing home to which many hunger-strikers were taken on release. In a professional partnership that reached its apotheosis during the war, they also founded the seven-bed Women's Hospital for Children in London's Harrow Road which also treated hundreds of out-patients. Here, both women honed their surgical skills. They would soon be preforming very different operations.

On 15 September 1914, Louisa and Flora were, like thousands of their male compatriots, on a train bound for France. Louisa was busily writing to her mother who, wishing she were twenty years younger, had waved them goodbye. Despite being skilled surgeons, they, like all female colleagues, had no experience of treating male patients. Nevertheless, they were heading to Paris where their newly-established Women's Hospital Corps (WHC) was to run a hospital for the French Red Cross in the magnificent (if ill-suited to its new metamorphosis) Hotel Claridge, Champs-Élysées.

The WHC was the result of a month's frenetic activity. Painfully familiar with the prejudice endemic in the British military and medical hierarchy, Louisa and Flora paid a call on the French Ambassador. He advised the Red Cross to accept their offer of this (unbeknownst to him entirely staffed by women) hospital unit. Intensive fundraising, another finely honed suffrage skill, followed. Within two weeks £1,523 (£160,000 today) had been raised, military-style uniforms ordered, and the initial steps that lead to Louisa and Flora becoming the British Army's first ever female surgeons were taken. Both believed, 'the militant movement had taught discipline and organisation; it had shown [women] new possibilities in themselves, and had inspired them with confidence in each other.'[17]

The disused, formally luxurious hotel, 'a gorgeous shell of marble and gilt without heating or crockery or anything practical but by dint of mild "militancy" & unending push' was transformed. The ladies' cloakroom, with its pavement access, its hot-water supply and basins, was converted into the operating theatre.[18] Claridge was soon admitting horrifically wounded British as well as French personnel. Chief surgeon Louisa and anaesthetist Flora, to the military medical authorities' amazement, proved as competent as male medics. Within a week of arriving in Paris with its all-female (many erstwhile militant suffragette staff), the Claridge 'was a smooth-running concern'.[19] Its reputation as one of the foremost military hospitals in France soon followed.

With the WSPU motto 'Deeds Not Words' as the WHC's guiding principle, Flora quickly drew visitors' attention to this hospital staffed entirely by women's achievements. 'Senior officers of the British Army seldom came to Paris without including the Women's Hospital in their rounds of inspection. Shown around by *médecin-en-chef* Murray and accompanied where possible by the Chief Surgeon, they saw the hospital "rose-coloured" through the spectacles of the doctors themselves'.[20] Sometimes the WSPU badges worn on all uniforms attracted comment allowing the suffragette medics to explain their case. Their 'facts and reasons' left at least one lieutenant colonel 'almost persuaded'.[21] The patients were equally enthusiastic, 'If I had the chance I'd give 'em ten votes apiece' declared one grateful Tommy. Even the anti-suffrage *BMJ* commented within a month, 'if this institution were the sole British hospital in Paris the medical profession in Great Britain might still continue to regard itself as well represented'.[22] This was made even more satisfying due to the *BMJ*'s frequent denial that forcible feeding was simply a humane and appropriate way to treat hunger-strikers.

Fighting a never-ending battle against wounds, Louisa became aware that mental injuries could be as severe as physical ones. She told her mother, 'Their minds are full of horrors and it is a help to them to come into a soothing atmosphere … All the men are shocked by what they have been through— and normal comforts and little pleasures are a help to them and make them sleep and forget a little.'[23] Flora felt women 'kept the human side' of medical and nursing care 'to the front'.[24] This care for 'shell-shocked' patients made a deep impression on Evelyn Sharp who visited the WHC hospital now established at Wimereux where staff showed 'a special understanding of … the psychology of their patients.'[25] Evelyn whose pacifism placed her in the 'uncomfortable minority', detailed the,

> irony of our civilisation, which first compels men to tear one another to pieces like wild beasts for no personal reason, and then applies all its arts to patching them up in order to let them do it all over again …. somehow, when the patching is done by women the ironic tragedy of the whole thing seems more evident.'[26]

It was a 'triumph for the militant movement, that these two doctors, who had been prominent members of the WSPU were the first to break down the prejudices of the British War Office against accepting the services of women surgeons'.[27]

The Wimereux WHC had been established following an interview at RAMC HQ in Boulogne. The Senior Officer told Flora and Louisa, 'We know all about the Women's Hospital Corps. Saw you in Paris. You are very welcome here. How many beds can you give us?' When their offer of 100 beds was accepted and 'surgery' requested, 'Their hearts leapt within them; for all the time it had been their ambition to see women doctors working as army surgeons under the British War Office.'[28]

The Wimereux hospital received a steady stream of official visitors and friends, the latter generally bearing comforts and delicacies for the patients including games, gramophones and on one occasion 'a car load of pheasants'. Although not listed amongst the official benefactors, the WSPU provided some financial support. One surgeon and patient embarrassingly recognised each other. She reminded him how he had 'once arrested me in Whitehall' to which he replied, 'with embarrassment … I wouldn't have mentioned it, Miss, we'll let bygones be bygones.'[29]

On 18 January 1915, with winter having rendered it almost unusable, Claridge closed. Flora and Louisa had 'set a standard which is quite unknown even among auxiliary hospitals … You are such a good example of what a hospital ought to be.'[30] Once it became apparent that Wimereux could be used as a casualty clearing station and with '50,000 additional hospital beds to be set up in England that spring', it was felt that the Corps 'could be of greater service in England than in France'.[31] Surgeon General Sir Alfred Keogh, a firm supporter of women in medicine, interviewed Flora and Louisa. Omitting to remind readers of the women's suffragism, *The Times* (19 February 1915) reported how, deeply 'impressed' by the WHC's work in Paris, Keogh 'had asked them to take charge of a hospital of 500 beds and if they pleased, of a hospital of 1000 beds'. The hospital in St Giles, Endell Street, an old workhouse recently occupied by Belgian refugees, was born; an arrival not greeted with universal acclaim. One RAMC colonel reportedly 'ejaculated, "Good God! … God bless my soul, *Women*!"' thereupon leaving the meeting perspiring heavily.[32] Ironically it was he who, the following month, handed over the keys to the RAMC's only hospital to be staffed and run by women (and partly funded by suffrage fundraising). This colonel and his side-kick captain, who were not alone in doubting Keogh's sanity, remained thorns in the women's flesh for many months. Disparagers gave the hospital six months at most before the women threw in the towel.

The exceptionally able staff included the 'brilliant pathologist Helen Chambers' with whom Louisa carried out high level research published in *The Lancet* (a rare accolade for a woman) and ophthalmic surgeon Amy Sheppard. The patients' claim that Amy had 'broken more windows than any other suffragette' – may be an exaggeration as, like many WSPU doctors who were dependent on their profession for their livelihood, she was wary of militancy preferring passive resistance including tax refusal.[33] Emmeline Pankhurst had shown genuine understanding of the medical women's dilemmas assuring them that by enhancing women's status within the profession, they were advancing The Cause. In a 1908 poll, of the 538 women doctors who responded ninety-seven per cent declared themselves in favour of women's enfranchisement.[34]

Although Keogh had been keen to appoint the women and gave them a military rank: Flora, lieutenant colonel (the only woman to hold the rank in the British Army) and Louisa, major, the War Office refused to give them badges of rank which soldiers would instantly recognise as symbols of authority, nor were they to be addressed by their titles. With their hands almost tied behind their backs, 'critics and sceptics [perhaps hopefully] prophesied that women would fail in keeping discipline', and to compound potential discipline problems (military hospitals are under military jurisdiction) only a newly appointed corporal was in charge of the RAMC detachment.[35] So good did he prove that he rose to sergeant major and, like all holders of that rank, dedicated himself to his duties, taking the hospital to his 'heart and often sacrificed Mrs Harris and his own leisure to its service' and, in the time-honoured tradition of sergeant majors, found ways to circumvent those 'wonderful and intricate volumes' King's Regulations, to aid the hospital's smooth-running. Whenever things went awry in another hospital, he would simply shake his head announcing, 'Nothing like that here, Doctor!'[36]

An unexpected ally proved to be the Officer in Charge of Barracks, both of whose daughters were suffragists. One belonged 'to a most respectable lot' but sadly, the 'other – she goes with Mrs Pankhurst's lot'.[37] Had the doctors ever heard of her? Seeing his men put to work by the (unsuspected by him) members of 'Mrs Pankhurst's lot' he felt sorry for them, 'Very energetic ladies! Oh! We are not accustomed to that in the Army.'[38] The 'energetic' ladies were also pioneers. Having run 'extensive, unique and highly successful trials using BIPP [an anti–sepsis] paste made of bismuth, iodoform and paraffin', in October 1916, Keogh stipulated its use as standard practice in army medical facilities.[39]

Concerns for patients' psychological wellbeing continued. Endell Street's bright atmosphere and focus on activities and entertainment lead the way in this aspect of patient care. Wards with flowers and brightly coloured blankets were designed to try to lift the gloomiest of spirits. Suffrage friends and colleagues were called upon to lend a hand and, reminding patients and staff of the hospital's suffrage links, the curtain covering the recreation room's small stage was embroidered with the WHC monogram and the Corps' motto, 'Deeds not Words'.[40] Opportunities to proselytise were grasped and towards the end of the war Keogh himself told Louisa, 'I think your success has probably done more for the cause of women than anything else I know of'.[41]

Not all staff shared their chief's suffrage enthusiasm. Writing home, Australian doctor Vera Scantlebury warned her parents 'I am in the midst of the very militant suffragettes'. With Australian women already enfranchised it may have been hard for 28-year-old Vera to understand English women's depths of feeling. However, she admitted that Flora, Louisa and others' lectures about women's achievements were interesting and some members of their audience were enthusiastic, and not only staff. Australian Private Crouch also explained in 1915, 'The whole hospital is a triumph for women, and incidentally it is a triumph for suffragettes.'[42] Suffragism was subtly apparent everywhere. Suffrage friends ran the library (suffrage books were on offer) including for a short while actress/author Elizabeth Robins (whom the authorities suspected of hiding suffragettes on the run from the police in her Sussex residence); another writer, Bessie Hatton, was honorary organiser and secretary of amusements.[43] So strong were the suffrage connections spread across the hospital that Vera sometimes signed off, '*Your Militant Suffragette*'. Despite her gentle mocking, as she grew to know the women, her admiration for them increased, admitting:

I have the greatest admiration and respect for these two women. They have struggled … and have succeeded beyond all expectations against the greatest prejudice.… From an old ramshackle of a place and against fearful odds they have made this hospital.… Our COs are wonderful brave hard-working women and their [*sic*] must be something in the cries for women suffrage if such women take it so seriously.[44]

Throughout her long and successful career as WHC commander-in-chief, Flora showed the flair for publicity associated with the suffrage campaigns. No photo opportunity was missed when the king and queen and other eminent personages visited. However, there was a frisson of anxiety when the Chief Magistrate Sir John Dickinson arrived as 'relations between magistrates and suffragists had not always run smoothly but he came in friendship with outstretched hand and kind congratulations'.[45] News about the hospital was readily available in the press, when casualties from the Somme were flooding into all hospitals, the 19 July 1916 society magazine *Tatler*, which had coined the term 'Suffragette Hospital', assured readers 'the noble ladies who manage the Suffragette hospital in Endell Street … are men in the best sense of that word, and yet women in the best sense of that word also'. A more gender-neutral article would have stated that all staff were medical professionals in the best sense of the word for, leading by example, Flora and Louisa ensured staff gave of their very best throughout the Women's Hospital Corps' life. Flora had warned them, 'You not only have to do a good job you have got to do a superior job. What would be accepted from a man will not be accepted from a woman. You've got to do better'. They proved that their abilities were at the very least on a par with, if not superior, to those of male RAMC colleagues.

Six women also gave their life, noted in 'Orders for the Day'. For example, 'It is with deep regret that I have to record the death on active service at this hospital of … She was our comrade and fellow-worker … she responded with courage and devotion to the call of her country.' Dr Elizabeth Wilks, mother of deceased Pathological Laboratory assistant 18-year-old Helen, assured Flora, 'Endell Street was the great time of her life. She loved the place … [her] last eighteen months were lived with intense enthusiasm and satisfaction', the same applied to all who served there.[46] When the war ended, the 'Suffragette Hospital' which against the prophesies of the jeremiahs had been a total success caring for over 26,000 patients, 24,000 of them male, would soon close.

Flora continued the feminist fight. In Spring 1916, inspired by Endell Street's remarkable success, Keogh had recruited 400 women doctors for service with the army. Following the passing of the 1918 Act and believing that MPs might now wish to curry favour with female constituents, she began campaigning for fair taxation for female military medics who enjoyed parity of neither rank, pay nor even tax status and attempted to bring the many iniquities suffered by colleagues serving with the RAMC to wider attention. Reverting to its former anti-suffrage tricks, *The Times* suppressed the ensuing correspondence, doctors then sent a circular to MPs listing their grievances.[47] Amongst the many inequalities, the women were taxed as civilians (at a higher rate) than their male colleagues. Flora's circular 'Bricks without Straw' sparked favourable responses; sixty-two MPs assured her, 'You may rely upon me and upon all future occasions to support the demand you make.'[48] The doctors then circularised the newly convened House of Commons requesting, amongst other items for consideration, Application for Relief under Service Rate of Income Tax by Women Doctors serving the War Office. Income Tax Act Schedule E allowed 'special rates of tax and scales of allowances to the pay' of those 'serving as members of any of the naval or military forces of the Crown'. Yet, women doctors were deemed ineligible for this relief. The Schedule having been brought to MPs' attention before the election, there was optimism that they would honour their pre-election promises and take up the doctors' case. They did not and only when the Naval and Military Sub-Committee intervened was fiscal parity achieved.

Parity elsewhere in the medical profession remained a pipe dream. Despite the overwhelming success of Endell Street, once its doors finally closed, the women were dispersed. The 'future was blank to the young girls who had been there so long and who were now to be unemployed'.[49] No glittering medical future awaited Flora or Louisa. Flora returned to private practice and to the Harrow Road hospital, now renamed the Roll of Honour Hospital; lack of funds forced its closure in 1921. She continued campaigning for universal franchise for the remaining two years of her life.

Flora's last years were not without controversy; she had refused the inclusion of the Endell Street Hospital in the Imperial War Museum's 'Women's Work Collection'. She argued that doing so would merge in the public's mind the only official hospital run by women and under the auspices of the RAMC, with 'other hospitals run by non-professional women'.[50] Another contretemps with the IWM occurred in early 1919. Official medical war artist Staff Sergeant Austin Spare had visited the hospital to draw an operation in progress. Despite being hung in the Royal Academy, Flora requested the picture be destroyed. She and Louisa considered that far from enhancing women's achievements as army surgeons, Spare had made 'their work look ludicrous to the technical mind'. Flora listed her complaints which she felt would 'indicate a serious professional breach of the most ordinary surgical practice'.[51] Whilst some might have rejoiced at the hospital being painted by so eminent a war artist, for Flora professional integrity took precedence. Anticipating the uphill struggle female surgeons would face in a post-war world rapidly revealing itself as misogynistic as the pre-war one, nothing should compromise the highest professional standards which women had set themselves and the WHC had achieved in Paris, Wimereux, and Endell Street.

Louisa died in 1943 and is commemorated on Flora's grave in Buckinghamshire. In *Women as Army Surgeons*, Flora refers to Louisa as 'Bold, cautious, true and my loving comrade'. Lord Knutsford commented, 'these women have done the impossible'.[52] His words serve as epitaph to these pioneer suffragettes who broke down barriers of misogyny and prejudice and proved to an initially disbelieving RAMC that women were more than capable of serving as Army Surgeons.

## Lady Londonderry (1878–1959) 'one of them 'orrible Army women'.[53]

Edith Chaplin was born with blue blood in her veins and a steel which the Women's Movement and the Great War would bring to the fore. Married in 1899 to Viscount Castlereagh, son of the 6th Marquess of Londonderry, she became one of the great political hostesses of her era. Unlike both her politician father and her mother-in-law, who compared Edith's political beliefs to those of 'a young hound running riot', she became an ardent albeit non-militant suffragist.[54] Lady Londonderry, whom Edith charitably refers to as 'an extremely able and brilliant woman', may have been unimpressed by the way that Edith had, by 1910, converted her husband to suffragism.[55] On the same day as reporting the events of Black Friday, *The Times* mentioned that Castlereagh had posed a question to Asquith in favour of Women's Suffrage.

Pro and anti-suffragists wrote numerous letters to newspapers as a way of engaging the public with their views. The anti-suffrage *Times* frequently refrained from publishing pro-suffrage letters but exceptions were made, particularly for members of the aristocracy, a position Edith exploited, never more so than in 1912 when the window-breaking campaign was at its height and misgivings about the policy, even amongst the militants, were palpable. Renowned, misogynistic scientist Sir Almroth Wright's views on 'militant hysteria' appeared in *The Times* (28 March). He outlined women's 'periodically recurring phases of hyper-sensitiveness, unreasonableness and loss of sense of proportion'. This proved women's unsuitability as electors. In 'The Unexpurgated Case Against Women's Suffrage', Sir Almroth (who vehemently believed there was no place for women in medicine, even less so for suffragette doctors), claimed there was much 'mental disorder' amongst the suffrage societies.[56] He offered a solution to a problem long seen to lie behind suffragism, namely 'Surplus Women', by which he meant unmarried adult women who should be sent to the Dominions, there to find husbands and fulfil their God-given role of wives and mothers! In the teeth of family opposition, Edith drafted a meticulous riposte which, to her mother-in-law's fury, *The Times* published on 1 April. In her autobiography she wryly comments that Wright's 'letter was the best exponent of a lack of balance, in an almost hysterical outburst against [women] in general', a point made on the same date by suffragist doctor and Harley Street specialist Agnes Savill.[57] Parenthetically, Edith's family was far from alone in being divided by the suffrage question. Sir Almroth's son, Edward, who died tragically in March 1914, left a legacy of £500 (£52,500 today) to the NUWSS.

Edith had other antis in her sights. In January 1913, her mother-in-law's friend, F. E. Smith had repeated the over-worked canard that 'as only Man could defend his country, only Man should have the vote'. She argued that Ministers of the Crown had recently demonstrated that it was men's rather than women's 'judgements and opinions [which were] coloured by emotional and personal considerations and might in moments of public excitement prove a source of instability and disaster for the State'.[58]

By 1914, Edith had not only honed her letter-writing skills; initially a nervous public speaker, 'nothing except the cause of Woman Suffrage would have launched me off as a platform speaker'.[59] She would also defend her position in tête-à-tête confrontations. At an August 1914 luncheon with mother-in-law,

> my recent 'goings-on' as they were called were challenged by the editor of a famous newspaper. He said that he would like to make a bet with me. I asked the purpose, 'Well, Lady Castlereagh,' he said 'it is this. I will bet you £5 that at the end of the war there will be no Suffragettes. War will teach women the impossibility of their demands and the absurdity of their claims'.

Having accepted the bet, her response was that 'he was right in saying that there would be no Suffragettes at the end of the war for we would have won our cause'.[60]

Like those of so many suffrage women, Edith's skills would be placed in the service of her country. Soon in uniform, which she wore continuously throughout the war, finding it liberating to not constantly have to change into the ever more elaborate outfits expected throughout the day of women of her class. 'I always wore uniform, and never before was life from the feminine standpoint of dress so delightful. You wore it at functions, you wore it for every day, at funerals or weddings.'[61] On one occasion, having arrived for a 'Society' luncheon in uniform, she was directed towards the Tradesman's Entrance. Learning her name, the unrepentant maid told her that she thought that she was 'one of them 'orrible Army women'.[62]

On 6 August 1914, suffragists Decima Moore and Evelina Haverfield founded the Women's Emergency Corps (WEC), subsequently the Women's Volunteer Reserve (WVR). 'The initial idea was that the Corps would register applicants for jobs such as cooks and interpreters [needed for work amongst the incoming refugees], for work in childcare, riding, driving and motor repairs.'[63] Overwhelmed by the number of applicants, in December 1914 Evelina asked Edith to become the Reserve's colonel-in-chief, with Evelina Honorary Colonel. Despite disliking the title which she considered misleading, Edith accepted. Scottish suffragette Dr Mona Chalmer Watson became honorary secretary. The WVR aimed to create a body of disciplined women to act as dispatch riders, signallers, telegraphists, motorists, and trench diggers. Comprising two sections, the Active Corps was for women aged between 18 and 50; the Auxiliary for either older women or those able to commit less time than 'Active' members. Training was on military lines, uniform was khaki and members undertook three drills a week. Although the WVR grew rapidly, Edith soon experienced significant doubts about the quasi-military lines on which it was run – angst about her own title had been well placed.

During the winter of 1914–15, 'abusive letters' flooded into the press about the Reserve's militaristic style and women 'masquerading' as men; Edith resigned, establishing her own 'breakaway organisation'.[64] With suffrage activism and suffragette violence still so fresh in the public's mind, she could understand that far from appearing praiseworthy, women's volunteering for wartime roles other than nurses and knitters was seen by some as an 'offence against God' and, probably more importantly, Man.[65] Many members whom she had recruited followed her into what became the Women's Legion (WL). When several women suggested that they would prefer the organisation to be known as the Women's Corps she humorously asked if they would really like shoulder titles inscribed WC? Along with WL shoulder-titles, a badge featuring Victory holding a Laurel Wreath and the motto *Ora et Labora* adorned their khaki uniform. Having avoided the WC shoulder-title, this badge was soon dubbed the 'Lady with the Frying-Pan' partly in acknowledgement of the many WL members who served as cooks. The WL became the largest single voluntary organisation on the Home Front.

Like many of England's upper-class women, Edith had links and contacts with men in positions of influence, and she too used these during the war both in the service of her country and to forward her own aims. Her feminine charms and beauty bewitched many of the top brass although one ruefully admitted, 'she cares not one jot for them or the others / She treats them all as if they were brothers'.[66] One *innamorato* was, conveniently, General Sir John Cowans, Quartermaster General; he proved a useful contact. Had she known of Constance Markievicz's advice to women about revolvers, she would have been able to heed it, in November 1914 she headed off to Boulogne with hospital supplies, to her delight, Cowans 'gave her a beautiful little Colt revolver'.[67] Like Evelina (who regretted not arming herself with her revolver on Black Friday), Edith was adept at handling rifles and shotguns.[68]

Safely back from Boulogne (the revolver still in its holster), in February 1915 Edith, now Lady Londonderry, called on Sir John and 'asked him if he would not consider having women cooks under their own women officers at camps, etc. [Four months later] he agreed'.[69] Initially used sparingly in convalescent camps, the experiment proved useful and cost effective; the women were paid £26 pa (£2,750 today) plus board and lodging. Constitutional suffragist Lilian Baker who had organised cookery classes at the beginning of the war and whose prodigious energy was always directed towards the good of her workers, was the first section leader.[70] When approaching Lilian, Edith quoted a note from a convalescent Tommy who had been fed by one of her trainees, 'After every meal, I thank God and Lilian Baker's cookery classes'.[71] Always leading by example, Lilian tested the mettle of socialites and working-class recruits alike and the replacement of male cooks and the improvements in standards of cooking moved rapidly ahead. A photograph of three young women held at the National Army Museum shows them wielding their weapons: rolling pin, ladle, and cleaver, with pride, their 'frying-pan' badges prominently displayed. Lilian's cooks were so successful that this section worked directly with the Inspector of Army Catering; they formed the nucleus of the Women's Auxiliary Army Corps, commanded in France by yet one more suffrage leader.

During the conversation with the editor who pontificated that by the end of the war the suffrage cause would be dead, Edith had 'contended that if and when a war took place, the role of women would be totally different from anything known in the past; that in future war would affect the whole community [and] women had only awaited the opportunity to prove themselves, and that our opportunity had come'. Having provided the army with female cooks and subsequently waitresses and gardeners, the next section comprised drivers working with the Royal Army Service Corps (they wore both RASC and WL badges).

As fortuitous a choice as Lilian Baker, Christabel Ellis became Motor Section Commandant in 1916. She too had excellent credentials in both peace and wartime. In 1908, she had come third in the first ever contest for 'Lady Motorists' held at Brooklands. Driving at sixty miles per hour, 'Miss Ellis lay almost full length on a sofa, with her toes within reach of the regulating pedals and hands ready for the brakes … With a true feminine touch, [she] had trimmed the "bonnet" of her racer [the Guarded Flame] with bunches of cornflowers and sweet peas.'[72] Parenthetically, suffragette WSPU driver Muriel Thompson the winner of this and other races against Christabel, had a distinguished war career. Decorated in the field by France and Belgium and Mentioned in British Despatches, she had had her Cadillac converted to serve as an Ambulance; in 1918, she became a recruiting officer for the Women's Royal Air Force.

With motor racing suspended 'for the Duration', Christabel initially drove ambulances in France (and possibly also in Serbia). Although the women of the Motor Transport (MT) Section of the WL did not draw the same rates of pay, they did identical work to the men, had charge of the same cars, worked the same hours with equal responsibilities driving anything from Generals to Peerless lorries. They took the same RASC MT test for cars, lorries and motorcycles. By the end of the war, they numbered several thousands. When in 1917 the Royal Flying Corps, (subsequently the RAF) called for women to replace men as drivers, they again responded. They drove through air raids, drove ambulances at night, met Ambulance Trains at all hours bringing home the wounded. Amongst their saddest duties was when the *Leinster* was sunk, WL drivers brought back traumatised survivors from Kingstown. As sometimes happened with all servicewomen and reminiscent of their suffrage experiences, 'they were also hooted and jeered at by hostile crowds and mud and stones were thrown at them. But they carried on quite unperturbed and cheerful.'[73]

A more cheerful reminder of their suffrage past occurred when a proud contingent of WL members, many of whom would have marched in their own processions including the Coronation one, formed part of the 'Procession of Homage and Address to the King and Queen on the occasion of Their Majesties Silver Wedding' in July 1918. Eleven months later, again led by Edith, WL members marched in the June 1919 Peace Procession. Edith believed that marching 'through the streets of London to salute their sovereign in the same procession with the men who had fought and won the war' was the 'Apex of achievement for all Service Women'.[74]

For some drivers, the war was not yet over as 100 of them accompanied the army of occupation to Germany; Edith proudly reported that despite the 'rudest of huts', the 'women never complained and took it all in the day's routine'.[75] Maybe there were a few for whom the rude huts were at least an improvement on the Holloway cells with their cockroaches and other vermin that a decade ago women had, not always successfully, complained about to the prison authorities. If a few were lucky enough to serve in Germany, most were rapidly demobbed. Having received fawning thanks from Cowans, it was soon obvious that women drivers were no longer wanted. Given one month's notice, they were 'requested to return all WL badges and Titles and any mackintosh items you have received, and your jerkin if not already handed in, and receipt for same held.'[76] As with so many of the women's Corps that had worked with the armed services, their assistance had been required – but strictly for the duration.

Having worked tirelessly for the Legion and with a constant feminist agenda guiding her writing of articles, speaking, interviewing, and seizing every opportunity to show that when given the chance, women could do almost any job as well as a man, Edith received the DBE in August 1917.[77] In January 1918 this was, to her delight, transferred to the military side to recognise that not only was the WL's primary object (in line with Emmeline Pankhurst's thinking) to free men to fight but that much of its work was directly military.

Edith's public service continued long after the war as did her commitments to disabled service personnel. Perhaps letting bygones be bygones, her old opponent, anti-suffragist Attorney General F. E. Smith appointed her as the first woman Justice of the Peace for County Durham. Celebrated in doggerel as 'a lady with a firm methodical push', this had carried her through the years when, believing in female suffrage, she had crossed swords with her mother-in-law and her own horse-obsessed Conservative MP father (who had finally been won over to Votes for Women when seeing the women of the Army Remount Department). It would propel her into continuing her suffrage work until the vote was won not just for the few but for all women, 'on the same basis as that possessed by men at the present day'.[78]

## Mona Chalmers Watson (1872–1936) and Helen Gwynne-Vaughan (1879–1967) 'Lord Derby wishes a woman of title. I want a working woman'.[79]

When in July 1915 the WL cooks went to the first army convalescent homes in Dartford, Eastbourne and Epsom, Dr Helen Gwynne-Vaughan, Head of the Department of Botany at Birkbeck University, was feeling increasingly anxious about her husband's health. A constitutional suffragist who was as interested in women's rights as female enfranchisement and not totally convinced by universal adult suffrage, she and her militant friend Louisa Garrett Anderson had jointly founded the University of London Suffrage League (open to male and female graduates). Helen had taken satisfaction in marshalling women into their places during the suffrage processions where she proudly marched under the University Graduates banner.[80] Unaware that this was preparing her for her future wartime role, she had, in a manner typical of one from her privileged background, long been involved with clubs for young working women.[81] 'Her benevolent autocracy was the complement of [working-women's] subservience, and each party found the required attitude in the other.'[82]

Her husband's death from tuberculosis in September left Helen facing a dilemma. She wanted to do 'something' but could not find war work which she felt would justify 'throwing up her employment and, as she considered herself in the same economic category as men, volunteering was not an option'.[83] As a botanist and bacteriologist, she longed to use her professional skills, 'I had visions of a mobile laboratory on some really dangerous front.'[84] This plan never materialised and she confided her ambition to Louisa. In a moment of serendipity and the inter-connectedness which marks many suffragists' wartime careers, Louisa put her in touch with her cousin, suffragette Dr Mona Chalmers Watson (the first woman to obtain an MD from the University of Edinburgh), sister of Brigadier General Sir Auckland Geddes, Director of Recruiting at the War Office and of Sir Eric Geddes, Director General of Transportation in France. Mona was doctor to suffragettes imprisoned in Perth.

The meeting between Mona and Helen, which would have such significance for women's first steps into the armed services, occurred because the British Army was facing a manpower crisis. The War Office had sought Sir Douglas Haig's views on recruiting women to work with the army in France in roles that would 'free up a man for the Front'. On 10 December 1916, Haig replied semi-favourably; he considered 'women clerks were less adaptable and generally less useful than men'.[85] Both Geddeses were involved in the discussions and in January 1917 Auckland arranged for Mona to present the ideas that she had drawn up for a women's corps to Sir Nevil Macready, UK Adjutant General. Meanwhile Florence Leach, head of the WL Housekeeping Section, had been in France with the express aim of establishing whether her members could replace RASC men and work in officers' clubs in army bases in France. Florence stressed WL members' desire 'to be under army discipline'.[86] Macready was initially not convinced; a firm anti-suffragist and loather of women's militancy, he believed an 'agitation is being engineered by those who run various women's organisations throughout the country'.[87] This comment was prompted by a NUWSS letter to Lord Derby advocating that the 'recruitment and control' of women in the army should be placed in women's hands.[88]

Macready's 'agitation' point was not unfounded. A Speaker's Conference on Electoral Reform had just concluded that some measure of woman suffrage should be conferred. Whilst the terms fell far short of the required universal female franchise, the NUWSS believed a Women's Army Corps would be 'a clear indication of the extent of women's participation in what had been a man's world; in the circumstances, could anyone have seriously argued that women should not have the vote?'[89]

With the unending manpower shortage, plans pushed on and in early February 1916, Mona explained to Helen that the Army Council was now considering forming a body of women for duty on the Lines of Communication where some 12,000 soldiers were currently doing jobs that women could almost certainly assume. This Women's Service Corps would comprise four categories both at home and overseas: cooks and waitresses; motor drivers and mechanics; storekeepers and clerks; workers with ordnance and with the RFC. With two young sons and her own professional life in Scotland, Mona was unwilling to serve overseas. Would Helen be interested in taking command in France with the rank of deputy commander? Whilst Lord Derby wanted a lady of title, Macready wanted a working woman. Helen, daughter of an officer in the Grenadier Guards, connected to Lord Saltoun whilst also being a university lecturer, ticked every box. An added bonus was that in the contemporary 'snobbish' world, Helen had made her social début at a Scottish ball attended by Sir Nevil Macready, then Adjutant of the Gordon Highlanders. Non-militant Helen was a married woman, which reassured Macready that she was not one of the so called 'inverts' he so feared. Impressed by Helen's charm and social ease, her 'little tricorne hat of black panne' clinched the matter.[90] The job, 'which seemed like the realisation of a dream' was offered.[91] She would demonstrate that it was not only her antecedents and sexual orientation that made her so admirable a choice for the post. Initially she and Mona were to be 'Chief Women Controller'. Furious at the insertion of 'Women', she charmingly pointed out to anti-feminist Macready that the title would be abbreviated to Chief WC, 'the charm worked'; she was now Chief Controller.[92]

Although the Women's Auxiliary Army Corps (WAAC) proved a resounding success, not all was plain sailing; some difficulties caused by Helen's enthusiasm and eagerness to over-militarise the role. She had spent time designing a uniform, 'khaki … the skirts most daringly short … twelve inches off the ground'.[93] Not all 'workers' (to Helen's disappointment military titles were not forthcoming,) were as impressed by the uniform as their Chief Controller. Clerk Ruby Ord remembered how women circumvented orders not to their taste, 'We decided amongst ourselves [what to do], … after all, we were suffragettes a number of us'.[94] The point is an interesting one, suffragists were accustomed to males in authority belittling them, now Ruby and other WAAC suffragettes were using their same skills to test female authority.

In July 1917, an Army Council instruction instituted the WAAC. For Mona, 'It is an advance of the women's movement and it is a national advance … Women have now a direct and officially recognised share in the task of our armies both at home and overseas.'[95] Mona dedicated herself to the early months of the Corps that had become dear to her and in August 1917 was gazetted CBE. When her son's ill-health forced her to resign in February 1918, the *Daily Sketch* applauded her for having 'organised and set going that most useful corps with conspicuous success'.[96] After the war, her commitment to feminist causes continued unabated. She felt 'It ha[d] been an honour to have lived through such great times for women, and to know that the generation after us will not have the same fight for liberty'.[97]

Although the new Corps and its Chief Controller faced inevitable teething troubles, by November 1918, just under 57,000 women had served in the WAAC with 10,000 serving in France. Helen herself ended the war in a different role. On 1 September 1918, 'sick and sorry', she had left France and the Corps she had lived with for nearly two years to take up a new appointment in England for which she had little enthusiasm.[98] 'With its early troubles behind it, the Corps had 'reached an established position [with] a recognised value. [Now] I was to leave them and begin again' as Chief of the WRAF to which she was appointed on 7 September 1918.[99]

On 27 June 1939, with another war looming and the QMAAC as the Corps was latterly known, having been disbanded eighteen years earlier, Helen returned to service as the Director General of the Auxiliary Territorial Service (ATS). Like all women's leaders' of the First World War, her guiding principle was once again to 'prove that women can do *anything* that they are asked to do'.[100]

## Chapter Four

# 'Votes for Women'? No Thanks!

### 'Represented by the Most Progressive and Enlightened Men.'

Having been constructed as largely muddle-headed, narrow-minded and dominated by male politicians, feminist historians have frequently overlooked one important aspect of the suffrage struggle. However, more recent scholarship has forced a re-appraisal and the admission that 'substantial numbers of intelligent, energetic women were committed' to a very different cause, that of anti-suffragism.[1]

Almost as soon as the campaign for women's enfranchisement began, some women as well as men declared themselves vehemently opposed to both women's enfranchisement and universal male suffrage. The opening salvo in the Anti-Suffrage Campaign was fired on 27 December 1906; Frances Low of Haslemere wrote to *The Times* arguing that women were already represented in Parliament 'by the most progressive and enlightened men'. By a strange juxtaposition of ideas, she added that if women entered politics, 'we shall see the same deterioration in political ideas that we have seen in those of newspapers which are written by and cater for women'. Like-minded women responded, on 15 January Sophia Lonsdale thought 'we should be doing something'; on 20 February, a committee was formed to promote an anti-suffrage petition. It collected 37,000 signatures 'in the quietest and speediest manner possible and was presented to Parliament'.[2] Well-known author Mary Ward, who published as Mrs Humphrey Ward, co-founder of Somerville College, Oxford (Somerville later disowned her) announced that in view of the 'spectacle of marching and counter-marchings of alarums and excursions on behalf of the suffrage cause in all parts of England' those who opposed women's suffrage should 'bestir themselves' to do something.[3]

At an inaugural meeting held on 21 July 1908 at the Westminster Palace Hotel, a Woman's Anti-Suffrage League was formed under the leadership of Lady Jersey. Membership cost one guinea (£115 today) for council members, 5s (£27.50) for ordinary members and 1s (£5.50) for associates – which would help fund the *Anti-Suffrage Review*. As well as Mary, high-profile members of the Executive Committee included Gertrude Bell – probably the 'brainiest' person in England, writer and reformer Ethel Bertha Harrison, her views that women's political activities would compromise their pre-eminent role as wives and mothers were shared by almost all League members. These women born into comfortable, frequently affluent homes, favoured women playing their part in local politics but considered national ones beyond (most of) their gender's intellectual capacities. They argued that as only men could take up arms to defend Great Britain and her Empire, only men were entitled to full citizenship. In time, some but not all antis would recognise that women's involvement during the 1914–1918 war was proof of women's citizenship. The contemporary firm belief in Britain's Imperial destiny was shared by most Britons and seemingly all antis; it was significant that the League's two chairmen were a former Consul General in Egypt (Lord Cromer) and, after Cromer resigned, the jewel in their crown, Lord Curzon, former viceroy of India.

Reporting favourably on the inaugural meeting in its leader column, *The Times* editor whose wife was an anti-suffragist, confidently agreed with Mrs Ward that the 'proposed changes [i.e. female enfranchisement] would be a disaster for England and first and foremost for the women themselves'; he concluded Mrs Ward 'is expressing the view of the great bulk of Englishwomen'.[4] Whilst both pros and antis claimed theirs as the majority view, it is probable that 'suffrage remained a minority pre-occupation across all social classes'.[5] Although the League lacked the WSPU's charismatic leadership, they scored some noticeable early successes including mustering 337,018 signatures for their 1909 petition – more than the suffragists ever managed.

Partly responding to the various men's pro-suffrage leagues, it was felt that a National Men's Committee for Opposing Women's Suffrage should be formed. This was little more than a list of names of men pre-eminent in all walks of public and cultural life including WSPU Edith Londonderry's father Lord Chaplin, and Gertrude Bell's father, Sir Hugh. In 1910, the two leagues merged as the Anti-Suffrage League (ASL) under Lord Cromer's presidency. Despite Gertrude commenting that he was the 'nicest man she had ever met', Cromer struggled to work with independently minded women who were now manoeuvred into lesser positions. Former President Lady Jersey was demoted to vice-president; she became a thorn in Cromer's side, lobbying for equal representation of women in key positions.

Following the merger, the ASL began 'to afford great delight and comfort to their opponents by the ineptitude and futility of their ways.[6] Unlike the pro-suffrage societies, the League received significant financial backing from some of the country's wealthiest bankers and captains of industry with Lord Rothschild their 'leading financial supporter'.[7] With such powerful backers, members had little need to become involved in the extensive and continuous fundraising undertaken by the various pro-suffrage societies which stood them in such good stead during the war.

Trying to match the suffragists' youth sections, a Girls' Anti-Suffrage League was formed. A private subscription ball was held which must have seemed tame in comparison to the WSPU's 'Young Hot Bloods' who had to be prepared to undertake the exciting-sounding 'Danger Duty' as well as singing nightly outside Holloway to keep up suffrage prisoners' morale. The Young Purple White and Green Club staged suffrage plays from which there were plenty to choose.[8] It is tempting to assume that Ruby Ord, the young WAAC who proudly proclaimed, 'we were suffragettes and used to breaking rules', was a former Young Hot Blood.

Like the suffrage societies, the ASL waged its campaign not only in its own *Anti-Suffrage Review* edited and largely written by Mary Ward but in journals such as *The Nineteenth Century* and the *National Review* as well as the national press. It was supported by many of local and national newspapers including *The Times*, the *Daily Mail* and what Millicent termed 'the three Posts' (*Birmingham, Yorkshire* and *Morning*) which unlike some papers 'remained anti-suffrage to the very end of our struggle'.[9] ASL members bombarded editors with cause-promoting letters, facts and figures and, unlike letters from suffrage women, these were generally published. In the light of *The Times* pre-war anti-suffrage stance (in 1912, Lord Northcliffe went so far as to tell Lord Curzon, 'my papers are going to do anything they can to support the Anti-Suffrage party[10]) the enthusiasm with which, on 15 November 1918, the paper thanked women for 'the invaluable services which they have so freely given to the national cause' strikes as being somewhat hypocritical. Although vigorous exchanges did occur in newspapers' 'Letters' pages, these could not compete with the drama and excitement of militant action, nor could the ASL propaganda leaflets and vicious cartoons telling women that they could not be 'spared for political life'.[11]

Nowadays with our constant availability of news from all sources, it is hard to fully understand the importance of organisations' magazines. These kept readers in touch, told of future activities, rallied troops whilst uplifting stories reminded women that they were united in a 'Common Cause'. Mary's sober eight-page small font *Anti-Suffrage Review*, which at times she wrote almost single-handedly, was the only anti-suffrage journal; it seemed 'stuffy' in comparison to the cartoons, witty articles and catchy headlines found in the plethora of magazines which catered for every nuance of the opposing campaign.

One similarity between the pros and the antis were the mass rallies and debates which provided future wartime speakers with significant practice in the art of public speaking which both sides continued to use effectively after August 1914. The most prestigious speaking event took place at the Royal Albert Hall on 28 February 1912; Violet Markham delivered a much-reported speech logically detailing her arguments against women's suffrage. Despite this success, 1912 was a year of tensions for the League; Cromer, referring to female colleagues as 'infernal women', resigned and a suitable replacement proved initially hard to find.[12]

The ASL never equalled the visual displays of the NUWSS or their even greater enemies, the WSPU. The League's popularity amongst working-class women was seemingly almost nil, and little better amongst younger middle-class women. In March 1912 a (perhaps biased) suffragist described ASL members as being largely rich and titled people with a high number of peers and their wives.[13] The crowds who flocked to watch loved the suffrage spectacle of gay and colourful processions in which all could 'March, March', belting out the inspiring suffrage songs.  Somehow the paid-for sandwich boards announcing ASL meetings in drab premises looked less appealing. Nor could the antis compete in the international stakes; suffragism was gaining worldwide appeal under the International Women's Suffrage Alliance which held conferences in international capitals including London in 1909. Maybe Curzon put his finger on the problem, he stated, 'there is nothing very exciting in defending the status quo'.[14]

As suffragette militancy increased, so too did the antis' vociferous condemnations. Constitutional theorist Albert Dicey told a friend, 'I am certain that with every pane of glass broken they will lose some 10 votes' or supporters.[15] During the militancy campaign, the antis easily occupied the moral high ground. Mary Ward's MP son Arnold condemned militancy as 'hysterical action' and should women be enfranchised, it would 'incorporate hysterical activity permanently in the life of the nation'. An upbeat Lord Curzon confidently assured the June 1914 AGM, 'the cause of the women's votes is absolutely dead in the present House of Commons'.[16] He believed their own militancy had defeated the Pankhurst and the WSPU's aims.

On the outbreak of war, antis did not face the dilemmas of many of their pro-suffrage opponents who agonised over their allegiances to Britain, to international suffragism or socialism; allegiances that would irrevocably destroy some friendships and split some families. For the antis it was more straightforward, it being man's duty to defend the Empire and woman's to stay at home and support him. They believed war would purge the nation of its weaknesses and comfortingly reinforce the gender distinctions which characterised what they considered to be 'advanced civilisations'.[17]

With war and a suffrage truce declared, the suffragists soon began (subtly) winning the propaganda war. Their well-oiled local press contacts ensured that inter alia, the NUWSS's Scottish Women's Hospitals for Foreign Service (SWH) featured in countless newspapers as did organisations such as the Endell Street ('Suffragette') Women's Hospital. Antis seemed unable to compete with, for example, the November 1914 *Ladies Field Supplement*'s elaborately illustrated account about the women of the Suffrage Movement's wartime work. To illustrate this point, the British Newspaper Archive's online search engine gave 720 hits for the SWH but a mere eighty-eight for the ASL. The antis' belief that they were fighting an uphill battle reminding the country that they too were 'doing their bit' seems justified. Even Gertrude Bell's crucial work in the Middle East did not carry the same appeal as women being decorated for gallantry in foreign fields. The antis' numerous war-workers were simply getting overlooked.

By 1916, the London Branches were justifiably demanding greater visibility. Antis too were in the thick of it. Beatrice Maunder Dormer's success with Lady Paget in Belgium was such that she was 'asked to establish a hospital for Belgian soldiers in Rouen', the Belgian king awarded her the Cross of the Order of Leopold in March 1915. Although no hint of their names has been found, apparently some anti-suffragists served with the SWH at Royaumont (and if at Royaumont no doubt on other fronts as well).[18] On the Home Front, Gladys Pott was striving to keep the nation fed and Ethel Colquhoun had established a free twenty-four-hour buffet for travelling servicemen at Paddington Station. The *Anti-Suffrage Review* furiously reported that the War Office had warned her against using the League's name in the buffet's title. Understandably, many antis felt that their opponents were now winning the media war, thereby gaining an unfair political advantage.

It could not have helped that the pros' old enemy Lord Northcliffe of *The Times* defected. In April 1915, he declared himself so impressed by the women that after the war he (and his papers) would be on their side – whether he remained so is a moot point. Mary Ward privately admitted to Curzon that they were almost certainly 'beaten'.[19] With militancy having been placed on hold for the duration, Lloyd George in the ascendancy, and Winston Churchill's star waning after the Gallipoli catastrophe, they acknowledged that partial women's suffrage would figure in the much-anticipated Representation of the People Act. In the light of die-hard anti Prime Minister Asquith having written to Millicent Fawcett in August 1916 praising women's war work, the antis' periodic suggestions that women war workers were neglecting their motherly and wifely duties sounded unpatriotic. By October 1916, although 'Mrs Humphry Ward and Lord Curzon stood firm … most of their followers had left them. Some of the chief women of their camp openly expressed a change of opinion, and men were deserting wholesale.'[20] With public opinion now undeniably in favour of Votes for Women, it is hardly surprising that when Lord Curzon stood up in their Lordships' House on that fateful evening in early January 1918, the policeman (as we saw in Chapter One) assured the waiting women, ''e'll do you no 'arm.'

## Mary Ward (1851–1920) 'Wandering into the Wrong Camp'.

In August 1914, Mary Ward's name was a household one, less for her prominent position in the ASL than for her eighteen novels, many of which had been 'best sellers'; although less commercially successful, her later novels kept the perils of suffrage activity in the public eye. Her popularity as a novelist was such that in 1908 she was invited to tour North America. Hosted by the Governor General of Canada, the friendship she formed with President Theodore Roosevelt would bear spectacular fruits between 1916 and 1919. Roosevelt had apparently only allocated the German Kaiser twenty minutes of his time as he had 'an appointment with Mary Ward'.[21] It was on her return from this tour that the Women's Anti-Suffrage Association held its inaugural meeting with 'Mrs Humphry Ward' as its head. Taking her position seriously, in her contributions to national newspapers including *The Times, Saturday Review, Pall Mall Gazette*, and the widely read *Nineteenth Century*, she aired her views that 'women are not naturally voters'; rebuffing detractors' claims about the narrow class appeal of the League, in the *Educational Review*, she asserted 'supporters are drawn from all classes'.[22]

The argument that it was her attempts to salvage her wastrel son Arnold's political career that propelled her into the ASL is compelling.[23] Born in 1876, the only son amongst three children, the apple of his mother's – and his spendthrift father's – eye, Arnold with his gambling addiction proved something of a rotten apple. In 1903, Mary's high hopes that he would become private secretary to the Viceroy of India Lord Curzon were dashed. In January 1910, after an uninspiring career as a lawyer, Arnold entered Parliament where he sat ingloriously until being de-selected before the December 1918 General Election. To his Imperialist mother's dismay, Arnold's wartime military career was, if anything, even more lacklustre.

Mary's importance to national life spread far beyond her writing, touring, or political views. Although she herself had not attended university, in 1873, whilst living in Oxford where her husband Humphry was a university tutor, she and two female friends had established a Lectures for Women Committee which, in 1879, led to the creation of Somerville (women's) College. Yet even this achievement would be overshadowed by her 1890 'Settlement' which she founded near St Pancras to try to ease the lot of London's poor. Initially called 'University Hall' this became the Passmore Edwards Settlement, Tavistock Square. (PES). This centre to which she dedicated so much of her time and energy, pioneered the importance of play in children's education and, another first, she forced a government commitment to the education of children with disabilities. Ironically, Sarah Carwin, nurse in charge of the invalid children's scheme, joined the WSPU, becoming amongst their most militant members and was frequently arrested and forcibly fed.[24]

PES also provided play schemes for working mothers' children which would prove invaluable during the war with weekly attendances running to a staggering 60,000.[25] With some commentators seeing Mary's work as laying the foundations of the Welfare State, it is sad that her anti–suffragism has overshadowed her significant contribution to improving women and children's lives.

Women on all sides of the suffrage divide were deeply committed to improving conditions for working women, mothers and children. There are close similarities between suffragettes Sylvia Pankhurst and Charlotte Despard's work in the East End and Mary's in St Pancras. Her 'reforming imagination, commitment to women's service and her literary depictions of women's friendship … lend weight to the argument that there was common ground' between the constitutionalist pros and the antis.[26] Thinking back post-1918 over their losing campaign, Mary's friend Janet Courtney felt 'we should have done better to turn ourselves into the right wing of the constitutional suffragists'.[27]

The PES, Mary's lasting legacy, was also the site of her greatest public humiliation. In February 1909, the antis challenged Millicent Fawcett to a public debate with Mary. Mary's side made a significant tactical error: with the debate taking place on home turf and believing that her eloquence would convince the undecided, they only reserved 150 of the 500 tickets for their own supporters. Mary's argument was that with the complexity of problems facing the Empire, men who 'bear the burden [of Empire should] be left unhampered by the political inexperience of women'.[28] Millicent calmly responded by pointing out that 'men were not intentionally neglectful but were so taken up in their affairs that the claims of women had little chance of attention'.[29] Mary, defeated by 234 votes to 74, realised that the opposition had produced better arguments. She changed tactics. Avoiding public debates with uncongenial speakers, henceforth she lobbied powerful men.[30]

Initially, the war work of Mary and her daughter Dorothy was identical to that of thousands of their age and class. Probably following an appeal from ASL colleague Gladys Pott, they organised female land workers for their local Hertfordshire Agricultural Committee, they tilled their own land, apparently daringly wearing breeches, and kept a weather eye on the PES.

It was in 1916 that Mary's contribution to the war effort changed spectacularly. On 27 December 1915, former President Roosevelt had written to her indicating that he felt the English case had not been well presented in America; people had little idea of what was happening both in England and at the Front. Through visiting the Front, could she help harness American outrage following the sinking of the *Lusitania* and counter President Wilson's reluctance to commit his country to the European bloodbath? Jumping at the invitation, Mary nevertheless decided that her travels had to be official and at the British and US Government's expense. Initially sceptical, the authorities concluded that 'after ten years of arguing the anti-suffrage cause, Mrs Ward was, without question, the most accomplished propagandist in England and, more importantly, she was the best-known Englishwoman in America.'[31] Only fools would fail to use her as Roosevelt requested.

*England's Effort*, a series of 'six letters' written to an 'American Friend', was published in 1916 – the title says it all. In purple prose, Mary explains how 'through the snow storms of this bitter winter' (1915/1916), she criss-crossed England: to the far north to visit the Fleet, to see the 'colossal' work of the factories incessantly churning out the weapons of war. Charitably in view of their diametrically opposed views about suffrage, she lauded the 'remarkable hospital in Endell Street, entirely officered by women; where some hundreds of male patients accept the surgical and medical care of women doctors, and adapt themselves to the light and easy discipline maintained by the women of the staff, with entire confidence and grateful good-will'; whilst the SWH in Serbia will 'rank as one of the noblest among the minor episodes of the war'.[32] Then, her greatest coup, an escorted visit to France where she and her daughter Dorothy, saw every aspect of England's effort.[33] Deeply moved by HMHS *Oxfordshire*, 'poor poor boys', a Casualty Clearing Station near Poperinghe with its 'tragic message of suffering, possibly death', she is elated to use field glasses to see the 'tower of Ypres … mute witness to a crime, that, beyond the reparations of our own day, history will avenge through years to come'.[34] Although nowadays, the style and language jar, *England's Effort*'s 'shrewd mixture of eye-witness reportage, statistical bombardment, telling anecdote and "beastly Hun" propaganda' and an epilogue on the 'squalid Irish uprising', was an immediate success.[35] Widely translated and even reviewed in the *Preussissche Jahrbücher*, she was jubilant.

Mindful of her success, in November 1916 she began lobbying to visit the French lines. With various hurdles cleared, Mary and Dorothy left

Charing Cross on 28 February 1917 on a train bursting with soldiers. *Towards the Goal*'s ten letters chronicle the differences she now espied in the machinery of war: aeroplanes like 'dragonflies' and '*Tanks!* The officer in front points smiling to a field just ahead. There is one of them—the monster!—taking its morning exercise'.[36] She also visited the Somme, scene of such devastating losses and, to her delight, was told (or at least thought she was) some so-called 'hush-hush' plans. Cleared by the censor, the ten letters addressed to a 'Mr R' appeared in American newspapers. The (not very) mysterious Mr R(oosevelt) wrote the preface to the book edition published in July 1917.

Mary had not abandoned her Anti-Suffrage commitments. On her return from France when it was now increasingly obvious that the antis were swimming against the tide of public opinion, Mary argued in *Anti-Suffrage Review* that suffrage women constituted only a small proportion of women active in war work and 'it is safe to infer that every No-Conscriptionist is a Suffragist'. The article's tone and March 1917 date make it tempting to see a link with the Wheeldon case.

With both *Towards the Goal* and her war novel *Missing* selling well, Mary's star seemed again in the ascendant, she felt at the epicentre of war and literary life. Her home life was less straightforward: Arnold had run up £6,000 (£477,600 today) of gambling debts which, to save him from being cashiered by his regiment, she had assumed.[37] In mid-1917, Arnold's application to join the tank corps was rejected – his poisonous reputation had preceded him. Mary fictitiously claimed that the anti-suffragists had recalled him to Parliament to assist their cause now facing imminent shipwreck with Lloyd George's proposals for women's enfranchisement. Did even her closest friends and admirers really believe that a serving officer would in wartime have been released to 'oppose the government of the land'?[38]

Even without the questionable benefit of Arnold's support, the antis were, by summer 1917, an obsolete rump. His last-ditch 20 June attempt at an Amendment to the Woman's Suffrage Clause was defeated by 300 votes. Only the Lords led by former viceroy Lord Curzon, whose private secretary Arnold had failed to become, could save them. Unbeknownst to the antis, the stage was set for the most significant defection of them all, Curzon's abstention in the Lords' vote. The defeat ended Arnold's parliamentary career. Despite the success of her wartime publications, Arnold's gambling debts and profligate life-style, and her husband Humphry's serious monetary miscalculations had almost bankrupted Mary.

Defeated in her political aims, unable to hide her son's fecklessness even from herself, Mary decided to turn her war publications into a trilogy. On 3 January 1919, she and Dorothy set off for foreign *Fields of Victory*, a 900-mile motor journey encompassing British, American and French front lines. Pro-Imperial and anti-German in tone, dedicated to the 'Allied Armies', there are poignant cameos which moved both the author and her readers deeply.[39] On her return she confessed that she had 'never yet come home with such an overwhelming impression of wreck and wrongdoing'.[40] Her mood was not lightened by either her meeting with President Wilson nor her audience with Sir Douglas Haig; did she know his kinswomen had been amongst the militant suffragettes?

On 11 March 1919, suffering from acute bronchitis, Mary Ward received a CBE. With so many of her erstwhile suffrage foes becoming Dames of the British Empire, her biographer believes that her January 1918 outburst against Curzon had been remembered, as perhaps had her continuous lobbying of him on anti-suffrage matters as late as November 1917. As a member of the War Cabinet, he may have felt that he had more pressing concerns than what was now the lost cause of women's suffrage. Like several prominent women from both sides of the suffrage divide, in February 1920 the lord chancellor invited her to become one of England's first women magistrates, a position in tune with her beliefs about women's role in the 'domestic' affairs of the country. Yet this appointment, her CBE and her honorary degree from Edinburgh University, seem 'poor reward' for someone who had achieved so much both 'for the children of the nation and the war effort' which included helping to bring America into the war.[41]

Mary's legacy is ongoing: the PES, now the vibrant Mary Ward Centre in Bloomsbury, offers over 900 different adult education courses to 5,300 daytime, evening and weekend students. It also helps Londoners access their legal rights.[42]

## Gladys Pott (1867–1961) 'I did not know how' to speak.

The seventh child and youngest daughter of the Venerable Alfred Pott, archdeacon of Berkshire, Gladys' family was devoutly Anglican. As befitted her social class, she was privately educated and acquired the art of meticulous attention to detail that became the hallmark of her life in public service. Despite sympathies with Victorian feminism, she became a staunch anti-suffragist. Like several colleagues, she 'contributed powerfully to contemporary debates over the nature of womanhood and women's potential contribution to national life'.[43] She espoused the contemporary 'separate spheres' theories which constructed women as 'angels in the house' with men suited to the cut and thrust of public and political life which included speaking on public platforms. Her early contribution to anti-suffragism was through letters to newspapers such as *The Times* wherein she picked holes in her opponents' arguments and rebutted their criticisms – unknowingly honing skills which would prove beneficial during the war.

'Spotted' by the League for her willingness to confront the other side and ask uncomfortable questions at WSPU meetings, she was invited to speak for the antis but protested 'I did not know how'. However, she quickly took to debating with leading suffragists including Millicent Fawcett. Gladys' speaking and organisational skills were propelling her to the forefront of the ASL as Lady Wantage explained to Lord Curzon, 'I can bear testimony to her remarkable ability and organising capacity and to her powers of speaking'. An acquaintance described her as a 'very able, good speaker, quite impressive, in fact a bit formidable … not particularly feminine'.[44]

In the 1910 General Election campaign, Gladys realised that she lacked Sylvia Pankhurst and Charlotte Despard's skills in countering suffrage propaganda in London's most deprived constituencies. She told Curzon, 'I have sent to Bow and Bromley all such workers as I can get hold of, both men and women, but they are a drop in the oceans of suffragists. It is too rough a constituency to ask ladies to work in except those used to Labour constituencies.'[45] Nevertheless empathising with those born to 'the tyranny of the cap and apron', she would in time become more comfortable negotiating and working with women from less affluent backgrounds.[46] Diarist Kate Frye saw Gladys as the antis' 'strongest ammunition'; having attended one of her lectures in December 1911, she considered her, 'a most harsh, repellent and unpleasing woman. She began by saying we should not get sentiment from her and we did not.'

One thrust of Gladys's argument, was that whatever suffragists claimed, the vote would not confer higher wages on working women. Eager to use facts to bolster arguments, she was the main author behind the 1912 anti-suffrage

*Handbook of Facts Statistics and Quotations for the Use of Speakers*. Aware that carefully marshalled 'facts' could not match the fire and passion of suffrage star-speakers inside and outside Parliament, she saw the need to hone speakers' skills, her own included. When Arnold Ward proved such an uninspiring Commons speaker, Gladys prepared notes to spur him on. In time, she and Ethel Colquhoun offered classes on public speaking. Suffragists were doing likewise, so that when war broke out, England had an army of polished female speakers, many of whom placed their skills at the service of the nation as they promoted various women's services.

By 1912, with the majority of MPs (if not the Cabinet) converted to female enfranchisement, antis had to demonstrate conclusively that this ran counter to what women themselves wanted. Gladys set about gathering the necessary evidence. As organising secretary of the North Berkshire branch, she claimed that out of the 1,291 female (Local Government) electors she had approached, 1,085 opposed the franchise, seventy-five were in favour and sixty-three neutral; presumably the remainder did not respond.[47] Canvassing four London boroughs achieved similar results. Although opponents called 'Foul' – she had included a reply-paid postcard (and as one *Times* letter implied, she had only canvassed those whose favourable replies she anticipated), the result crucially restored the League's credibility in some MPs' eyes. In February 1914, armed with her statistics, she had pro-suffrage Lord Cecil in her sights. She was increasingly confident about crossing swords with the highest profile men in the land.

Forthright in all her views, archdeacon's daughter Gladys sought to expose the militant suffrage connections of 'the ridiculous League which calls itself the "Church Suffrage League"'.[48] By 'slipping a word to the Archbishop of York', her anti-suffrage colleague Gertrude Bell had, in 1912, prevented a suffrage question being discussed at the Middlesborough Church Congress, nevertheless, Gladys felt that anti-suffragists should remain vigilant against the church being usurped and exploited by fanatics. She helpfully provided Curzon with facts and figures to use as ammunition. She deduced this 'Church Suffrage League' is almost certainly the 'Church League for Women's Suffrage' formed in 1909 to 'band together on a non-party basis, Suffragists of every shade of opinion who are Church people in order to secure for women the vote in Church and State'.[49] (Post-war these Leagues campaigned for the ordination of women.[50]) By 1912, 'nobody doubted the great organising ability and importance of Gladys Pott' who had become the ASL's secretary.[51]

Gladys did not see the ASL through her friend Mary Ward's rose-coloured spectacles. She was aware that despite many of the key national dailies' anti-suffragist views, other editors were more ambivalent, even favourable, and that the oxygen of publicity kept suffragism in the public's mind. She impressed upon Curzon the need for the League to pay more attention to press work and propaganda, even at the expense of Mary's *Review*. Better parliamentary liaison staff and a stronger, more active committee to give its attention to press work were essential. 'I desire to place on record my own firm convictions that publicity in the Press is our greatest need and our opponents' chief advantage over us.'[52] Her constant letters and comments in newspaper showed her practising what she preached. Despite Gladys's and others' best attempts, by 1913 the antis were fighting a rearguard action with internal divisions, perhaps aggravated by the ineptitude of 'their' MP, Arnold Ward now apparent.

In August 1914, Gladys, who had fought so hard for the ASL, placed her anti-suffragism on hold. Like those she had fought with and those she had fought against, she discovered that the talents and skills she had acquired would admirably serve her nation. Her personal contribution in getting women on to the land, initially by promoting rural women's involvement with agriculture, subsequently with the Women's Land Army formed in 1917, has been undeservedly overlooked.[53]

Although an army marches on its stomach, civilians also need feeding but, initially, the government was complacent about the nation's food stocks; with the war going to be 'over by Christmas', the best thing to do was not panic and bring the harvest in. The NUWSS advised women to get in touch with local farmers and volunteer their services, on a temporary basis. Local papers soon featured reports and images of women 'following the example of their French sisters' and doing their harvesting bit.[54]

1914's harvest was saved but by December things were looking more serious; many agricultural labourers had enlisted and women seemed unimpressed by farm work. Despite Emmeline Pankhurst's 'Right to Serve' March featuring land workers and cuddly lambs, recruitment remained stubbornly low. In autumn 1915, County War Agricultural Committees, and Women's War Agricultural Committees (WWAC) were established;

Gladys Pott's name appears as Treasurer of the Berkshire Committee of Women and Farm Labour; she was also closely involved with Bedfordshire. Accurate figures for village women land workers are notoriously hard to come by; Bedfordshire, is the exception, 'extant records of the committees that supervised the organisation of women's work on the land [here] are unusually rich'.[55] Tempting to see here the hand of the meticulous Gladys.

From the early days, certain ministers and women's leaders had stressed how Frenchwomen undertook most agricultural labour, now Englishwomen must emulate them. A group of eight handpicked women would travel to France to observe and report favourably on all that they saw. Gladys was selected, alongside 'anti' Sarah Boyce from Gladys's home turf. Wife of a smallholder and village fishmonger, Sarah's diary of her 24 February – 5 March 1916 trip is fascinating, more for her excitement at being abroad than for her farming comments.[56] Despite terrible weather, ubiquitous cemeteries, and the proximity of Verdun ('we can hear the guns!!') which had, unfortunately to Sarah's mind, started just before they left England, thereby reducing their itinerary, the women found the tour informative. Gladys's detailed report in *Reading Mercury* and Sarah's and Gladys's ensuing speeches in Kensington show her drawing on her former anti-suffrage skills to gain maximum coverage for the 'plucky band of women' and their fact-finding tour.[57] In March 1915, the visit is referenced twelve times in *Reading Mercury*, one anti-suffrage letter is also published. The travellers were determined to 'rouse our own village women to a sense of their duties in connection with labour on the land'.[58] This high-profile trip allowed Gladys to counter some of the media attention that the suffragists seemed so good at attracting; as early as December 1914, she had wanted to show that anti-suffragists were also deeply involved in war work.

Despite many rural women's herculean efforts, the food situation was increasingly critical. Now the Bedfordshire WWAC began organising the recruitment of women for the newly formed 'Women's Land Army' (WLA) under the National Service Scheme.[59] In early February 1917, Gladys's appointment to the WLA was triumphantly announced in a local paper. She was organising a short six week 'crash course' providing women with rudimentary knowledge and 'an insight into the kind of jobs [they] will be expected to undertake on a farm', and also designing uniforms consisting of 'a very short skirt or tunic over thick stockings and heavy boots with gaiters or puttees [and] knickerbockers'.[60] The seemingly superfluous skirt was to remind the wearer that she was feminine despite being engaged in the so-called 'food war'. Yet numbers remained stubbornly low. In February 1917, writing in her role as a 'Travelling Inspector' under the women's branch of the Board of Agriculture and Fisheries, (a post she would fill between 1916–19), Gladys noted 'Munition making [of which she was never a fan], hospital nursing, canteen management and the like all appear to be directly connected with the Army organisation, and to be essential to the prosecution of the war. They therefore possess a glamour and attraction which is absent in Agricultural work.'[61] Her old anti-suffrage public-speaking skills were now pressed into service as she led and spoke at meetings successfully appealing to women and girls to 'Save the Harvest' – which they successfully accomplished in both 1917 and 1918.[62] Her countless wartime public speaking engagements indicate that Gladys, who once shied away from public speaking because 'I don't know how', had been transformed into an accomplished and confident 'star turn' with facts and figures at her fingertips, used in both meetings and newspaper columns.

With the suffrage battle lost and the food war (as well as the Great War) won, a new career opened up. Seen by politicians as a 'safe pair of hands' who had never sought to challenge the established order, in 1920 Gladys was offered the chairmanship of the Society for Overseas Settlement of British Women (SOSBW) which aimed to facilitate the post-war emigration of 'surplus' British women to the Dominions where they would, it was hoped, start a new life and, by marrying colonial men, re-stock the Empire. This appealed to Gladys's Imperialism. However distasteful the organisation sounds to modern ears, many contemporaries felt it offered women genuine opportunities; wartime land-workers were amongst the early prime targets.

Imperialist Gladys remained a 'driving force' in the SOSBW until her retirement in 1936.[63] Still an accomplished speaker, at her farewell address, she stressed her continuing commitment to 'the most wonderful flag in the world'. By helping 'to distribute women who would carry with them these traditions of political and social sense into the homes of less populated parts of the Empire,' she believed the Society had played a part in maintaining the values for which the Great War had been fought and which the rise of dictatorships was ominously challenging.[64] Appointed OBE in 1926 and

CBE in 1937, she would live long enough to see a new generation of Land Army girls win the food war the second time around.

## Violet Markham (1872–1959) 'the most uncongenial task to which I ever set my hand'.

For Violet Markham, the 'lines of life ha[d] fallen in pleasant places'.[65] The youngest of five children of a staunchly Liberal, Derbyshire coal and iron magnate, her mother's (and subsequently Mary Ward's) influence led her towards anti-suffragism. Like many socially privileged unmarried women, she became involved in 'good works'. With women now entering public life, her election to the Chesterfield School Board was in keeping with her belief in women's importance to local government which extended women's domestic role into the home life of the nation.

She visited Egypt in 1895 becoming friendly with the then Consul General Lord Cromer; she moved easily amongst the great and the powerful. Her travels and friendships led to a staunch commitment to the British Empire – as well as an ability to use acquaintances and contacts to further her aims. Following a 1901 legacy, she established a Chesterfield Settlement, then moved to 8 Gower Street, London, becoming Millicent Fawcett's neighbour. Like so many women on both sides of the suffrage divide, she was appalled by women's sweated labour and atrocious working conditions, concerns that would stay with her throughout her public life. However, she disagreed that the franchise would improve women's lot; furthermore, she argued, universal suffrage would simply increase the number of ill-educated voters. Bizarrely for someone who had travelled across the British Empire, she informed the ASL's inaugural meeting at Queensgate Hall, Kensington, that Imperial understanding was beyond a woman's intellect.[66] The *Derbyshire Daily Telegraph* proudly reported the arguments of this 'remarkably clever [Derbyshire] woman', assuring readers that she could 'hit hard', would undoubtedly give Christabel Pankhurst a run for her money and then, ambiguously, 'few women have more right to the vote on the score of intelligence'.[67] By 1910, she was co-chairing meetings with the big anti-suffrage names, including Cromer and Sir Hugh Bell. Suffragettes' heckling bothered her not at all.

Violet's big breakthrough occurred at a major anti-suffrage rally at London's Royal Albert Hall on 28 February 1912. Acclaimed as THE speech of the evening, and published in leaflet form, more than one commentator felt she had made 'so admirable a speech against the enfranchisement of women that she nearly defeated her own cause'.[68] Drawing 'blood from my suffragist opponents', the antipathy directed towards her meant that, for a few days, she was 'under police protection'.[69] Sylvia Pankhurst called her a 'foul traitor who while suffragettes were hunger-striking appeared on the Albert Hall platform surrounded by reactionaries like Lords Cromer and Curzon protesting against women having the Vote'.[70]

In a 1913 letter to Lord Cromer when militancy was at its height, Violet expressed concerns about 'the prevailing anarchy in my sex', bewailing 'the sort of loose spirit which seemed to have come over the relations of men & women'.[71] Nevertheless, by 1916, those whom she had once supported now also considered her a 'foul traitor'. Her wartime work had propelled her into the opposite camp. Suffragism appears her more natural home, she had once confessed anti-suffrage work was 'the most uncongenial task to which I ever set my hand. I love & honour my own sex, & it's odious to seem in opposition to them.'[72]

Whatever her pre-war thoughts about men and women's separate spheres, the Shell Crisis crystallised Violet's views about women contributing to the war effort; 'no effort can be too great to meet the emergencies with which we are confronted'.[73] England's need was paramount. If women were required in the factories, then into the factories they should go, be paid fair wages and given a place on negotiating bodies. The first statement was popular with 'anti' colleagues, the subsequent ones less so. Many antis saw well-paid workers as a threat to the pre-existing social order.

Trying to explain her 1916 defection, Markham told Cromer 'the man as worker, the woman at home remains my ideal of society. But in this difficult world … little though I like it, women are going to play an ever larger part in industry and public life.'[74] Violet herself would play a significant part. A National Service Department (NSD) was launched in February 1917 to ensure war industries were supplied with appropriate workers but this was plagued with difficulties from the beginning.[75] Violet was appointed Deputy Director of the Women's Section which, like the men's section, aimed to send (women) war workers wherever they were needed. Resigning six 'odious' months later, she saw this NSD as a 'fiasco' (largely due to Neville Chamberlain's ineffective leadership) although she accepted that the women's section had been an 'island of harmony floating on a sea of discord'. The bitter experience taught her, 'how little a man's position may correspond with his real merits'.[76]

A different role awaited her. In France, Helen Gwynne-Vaughan's WAACs had hit stormy waters. 'Scavengers in rumours' dustbin' were circulating accusations of 'gross immorality', the newspapers were having a field day and recruitment plummeted.[77] A Commission of Inquiry was set up to investigate with Violet appointed Hon. Secretary. Commissioners spent 'eight exciting days in France, some of them sufficiently near the front-line for us to feel the atmosphere of battle'.[78] More importantly, amongst over 6,000 women, 'we found few signs of immoral conduct'. Soon Violet herself would be accused of 'immoral conduct'. Although Helen was privy to the information, relatively few people knew that Commissioner Miss Markham had married in 1915. Whilst on her inspections, she and her serving officer husband stationed in Montreuil, had 'snatched' a short while together. The WAAC officer who came to announce dinner was outraged to find 'a large officer sitting on Miss Markham's bed while Miss Markham in a *négligée* was doing her hair'![79] Explanations of her married state fell on largely deaf ears; rumours abounded about 'That Miss Markham'. Violet saw the funny side of the morality commissioner being accused of immorality, concluding that 'a little mirth was welcome for the times were not gay'.

In December 1918, this once staunch anti-suffragist unsuccessfully stood for Parliament. Canvassing in Mansfield, she was touched by the 'generosity of spirit' of an erstwhile suffragist opponent, Eleanor Rathbone, who had 'every reason to regard me with dislike' yet joined her on the campaign trail.[80] Like other prominent war workers on both sides of the suffrage divide, Violet was appointed JP, subsequently Mayor of Chesterfield. Deeply involved in both charitable and government work, during the Second World War she again found herself investigating servicewomen's morals – accusations which, to her satisfaction, once again proved unfounded.

## Gertrude Bell (1868–1926) 'Major Miss Bell'.

The eldest, most beloved daughter of England's sixth wealthiest and most successful industrial family, Gertrude Bell was endowed with intellectual abilities that overshadowed most of her generation. The range of Gertrude's achievements is breath-taking: the first woman to achieve a First Class

Honours degree in Modern History from Oxford, she had locked horns with the examiners in her public viva voce examination; owning no trousers, she had scaled Mont Blanc in her underclothes and even had a mountain peak, the Gertrudspitze, named after her. Partly as an attempt to 'feminise' her after the intellectual sparring of Oxford, her parents organised for her to travel across Europe and beyond. By the beginning of the century, her intrepid explorations of the Arabian desert had earned her worldwide renown. It seems somehow surprising to find her named as Honorary Secretary to the Women's Anti-Suffrage League at its July 1908 inaugural meeting.

Gertrude's involvement with anti-suffragism was not without reflection. Despite frequently discussing the 'suffrage question' with her stepmother Florence's close friend, WSPU actress and author Elizabeth Robins, Gertrude remained unconvinced. One argument used to counter women's claims to enfranchisement was that their husbands or fathers would always vote with their womenfolk's interests at heart. Nothing in Gertrude's life would have led her to doubt this comforting panacea. With a doting father who pandered to and financed her every whim, she saw working-class women as a species apart. Despite some involvement with Florence's philanthropic endeavours, she seemed unable to comprehend these women's desperate poverty and harsh lives. Her 'lack of humility and lack of self-criticism disallowed her from adopting a more balanced view', nor, as an Imperialist, could she contemplate these women holding the fate of the Empire in their collective hands.[81] Although she subsequently seemed to suggest she felt 'obliged [by Lady Jersey] into becoming honorary secretary', she may in reality have been, as Lady Jersey latterly implied, an eager founder member of the League.[82] Exploring the Middle East, Gertrude had faced off marauding Bedouins and knife-wielding desert raiders and ventured with impunity into areas where no white woman's foot had previously trodden, it seems improbable that even Lady Jersey could have forced her into taking a position against her will. She was certainly a high profile catch for the 'antis' and entered the suffrage debate with her characteristic 'zest'.[83] Her letters to *The Times* would be noticed.

Within four weeks of the inaugural meeting, Gertrude was in confident mood assuring *The Times* editor on 20 August that a 'territorial army of Amazons … will be needed to retard the progress of a society so successful as the Anti-Suffrage League has proved to be'. On 13 October, feeling 'the controversy has now reached a critical stage', she urged all who shared the League's views to waste no time in enrolling as members. She practised what she preached. En route for the Middle East, her 21 January 1909 diary entry reads, 'My travelling companion was a Mrs Broadbridge, an intelligent little woman wife of an engineer who is now on the W[est] coast of Africa. She had been all over the world. We talked of the suffrage and I enlisted her among the Antis.'[84]

Between 1909 and 1914, Gertrude's life took a different direction to her anti-suffrage friends. Interested but perforce from a distance, she was now plunging into political whirlpools across the Middle East. A polyglot whose numerous languages included Arabic, Turkish and Persian, she perfected her mapping skills (these would be very beneficial to T. E. Lawrence, by his own admission a poor, lazy cartographer who invented what he couldn't be bothered to investigate), excavated numerous archaeological sites some never hitherto explored by a woman (it was here that she first met Lawrence), visited harems, and, 'with a haughty air of self-assurance' travelled as a lone woman deep into the desert – accompanied by an impressive cavalcade of accoutrements including a rubber bath and a full dinner service, and she was occasionally imprisoned.[85] Her love for and understanding of Arab tribes who were chaffing against the continuing Ottoman rule and which she believed could be used to Britain's advantage, would have far-reaching consequences not only during the Great War but to this day. It was she who warned that tensions between Sunni and Shi'a would ultimately spiral out of control. Having noted the Turkish–German built railway which would come to threaten England's control of the Gulf, she shared her views with Britain's Ambassador to Turkey, he 'immediately wired Foreign Secretary Edward Grey', who knew the Bells socially.[86] Back in England in May 1914, Gertrude was a rare female recipient of the Royal Geographical Society's prestigious Gold medal.

At her parents' home when war was declared, she immediately encouraged her father's workforce to enlist and the first act that would lead to her playing a crucial part in Military Intelligence was about to occur. Asked for a full report on what she had 'learned in Syria, Iraq and Arabia', the 'Bell Report' was forwarded to the Director of Military Operations in Cairo and thence to Sir Edward Grey.[87] She advised organising the Arabs in a revolt against their

Turkish overlords and pleaded for permission to return to the scene – which was refused being 'too dangerous for a female'.[88]

Instead, armed with a passport which gave her profession as 'none', in November 1914 Gertrude began working for the Red Cross in Boulogne. Undeterred by Army obfuscation and showing her usual talent for cutting through red tape, she soon created a Wounded and Missing Enquiry Department, discovering 'I have inherited a love of office work! A clerk was what I was meant to be'.[89] However talented an administrator, this was poor use of the specialist skills and knowledge of Britain's greatest expert on the Middle East, beloved and trusted by almost every key Arab across the region.

Gertrude's private life was now in turmoil. In love with the married Major 'Dick' Doughty-Wylie whom she referred to as 'heart of my heart', the mores of the time made any relationship impossible. He was destined for the Dardanelles which she rightly believed 'has grown into a very big, if not impossible business.[90] Back in England, having just written one of many letters to him, 'Since I've heard nothing of you I conclude you are all right & I'm cheerful again, after some days of wild anxiety', on 1 May 1915, she learned at a London dinner-party that 'Dick' was dead. Unable to speak openly of her grief, neither her work for the Wounded and Missing nor her subsequent job of creating lists of POWs and internees in Germany could ease her pain.

In the depths of her mourning, she received a summons: the War Office had suddenly awoken to the fact that 'anyone can trace the missing but only I can map Northern Arabia. I'm going next week'.[91] Boasting a feathered hat, greeted by T. E. Lawrence, on 26 November 1915, 'Major Miss Bell' arrived in Cairo, bursting upon the Military Intelligence scene. Life for the occupants of this erstwhile backwater (soon to be renamed Arab Bureau) would never be the same again. Following the Gallipoli debacle, the Bureau's focus was now Mesopotamia, Arabia and the Gulf. Success here would depend upon the Arabs; would they align themselves with the unpopular but fellow Muslim Turks or the more popular but infidel British? With her unparalleled knowledge and understanding of these areas, could Gertrude provide the answer to the conundrum? Taking over from Lawrence, she began meticulously cataloguing the Arab clans' loyalties and political alliances. In January 1916, she boarded a troopship heading to India to enlist Viceroy Hardinge's support and financial aid for an Arab uprising which would thereby destabilise Turkey. She became officially part of the India Expeditionary Force 'D' with pay but 'fortunately I need not wear uniform'. As she told her father in May 1916 after transferring to Basrah, it was her deep friendship with so many leading Arabs 'which makes me useful now'. The antipathy directed towards her for being a woman was overcome. If anyone could encourage an Arab uprising against the Turks, it was undoubtedly Gertrude. Hardinge's warning that she is 'a remarkably clever woman with the brains of a man' was intended as a compliment and doubtless accepted as such.[92]

Reminiscent of her contributions to the ASL and to the Wounded and Missing Bureau, Whitehall considered Gertrude's incisive reports about the Arab situation to be the 'clearest and most readable of all the official documents that the Arab Bureau produced'.[93] Her CBE awarded in October 1917 was greeted with effusive delight by former fellow anti-suffragist Beatrice Chamberlain, although Gertrude herself claimed not to 'care a button about these things'. Parenthetically, her stepmother who turned the family mansion into a hospital received a DBE. Often seriously ill, at times deeply homesick, constantly seeking to enlarge her understanding of the Arab world and the contributions this could make to Britain's cause and the Arabs' future wellbeing, for Gertrude the war ended in Iraq.[94] With Baghdad 'in a ferment' due to the Franco-British Declaration, Gertrude was privy to Arab leaders' thoughts and anxieties for the future, warning 'the whole situation requires very delicate handling'.[95]

Deeply critical of the Sykes–Picot treaty and Lord Balfour's Declaration, 'if only people at home would not make pronouncements how much easier it would be for those on the spot',[96] she attended the March 1921 Cairo Conference on the Middle East; she accused Lawrence of circulating 'lies' about the British in Mesopotamia.[97] Churchill eventually accepted her and her (in-name-only) Chief, Sir Percy Cox's advice that Britain maintain a presence in Iraq by establishing an Arab regime advised by British officers. In 1920 she was influential in securing the Iraqi throne for her protégé Faisal ibn Hussein and determining the nascent state's boundaries.

With Faisal securely on the Iraqi throne and her cultural success as Honorary Director of Antiquities of the Iraq Museum in Baghdad which she had established, she was noticeably depressed and lonely. In the evening of 11 July 1926, she fell asleep with the aid of sleeping pills. Political Officer

Frank Stafford publicly declared she had 'died of natural causes', privately he concluded that the evidence 'pointed to suicide'.[98] Buried with full military honours in Baghdad's military cemetery, George V assured her parents that the nation mourned the loss of 'her intellectual powers, force of character and personal courage'.[99]

On 14 July 1926, Colonial Secretary Leo Amery 'paid her the rare tribute' of a statement in the House of Commons, that hallowed ground from which she had sought to exclude women. Britain had 'lost not only a most valuable public servant, but also a remarkable and indeed unique personality' whose 'intimate knowledge of the East enabled her to render exceptional service to the British Forces'.[100]

Yet the mourning proved short-lived. Now largely overlooked in mainstream histories of the Middle East in the Great War, a recent biographer noted that 'In the basement of the Iraq Museum, on a forgotten shelf, the bronze bust of Miss Gertrude Bell waits to be dusted off.'[101] With Gertrude written out of David Lean's 1962 film *Lawrence of Arabia*, in 2015 the biopic *Queen of the Desert* sought to redress the balance. Yet Nicole Kidman's comment that her character Gertrude Bell was 'the female Lawrence of Arabia' distorts the truth. Despite his renown, Lawrence's empathy with and standing amongst the leaders of the Arab world was only ever a poor second to that of Major Miss Bell.

*Chapter Five*

# 'I tried to stop the bloody thing!'

## 'The fate of Europe depends on decisions which women have no power to shape'.

The story of the suffrage women who sought to prevent the war, who tried to retain contacts with women across all combatant nations throughout the war, and who refused to work for the war effort, sits ill within the popular if not totally accurate narrative that it was women's war work which earned them the vote. But, like overlooking the anti-suffrage campaigners, hiding these so-called 'peacettes' from history impoverishes the nuanced story of suffragism and the Great War.

Another popular British misconception is that Votes for Women was a British phenomenon. This is far removed from the truth as many countries had their own suffrage movements. By 1902, leading suffragists, feeling that more needed to be done to coordinate the national movements, formed an International Woman Suffrage Alliance (IWSA) in Washington, USA. This would act as an international body to help stimulate and support various national organisations' quest for women's citizenship. Millicent Fawcett, elected as a vice-president *in absentia*, led the British delegation at the inaugural congress in Berlin in 1904. Regular congresses took place. The 1909 London one was the most spectacular, using well-honed skills, militants and constitutionalists staged eye-catching 'displays of sisterly solidarity'.[1] The representatives of the twenty-six affiliated associations who attended the 1913 Budapest Congress, looked forward to meeting in Berlin in 1915. Women's suffrage had become an international movement.

In 1914, IWSA secretary Hungarian-born Rosika Schwimmer moved temporarily to London. Well known as a skilled lecturer on feminist topics, when attending the 1909 (London) Congress, she became the first foreign woman to address the House of Commons Foreign Affairs Committee.[2] On 11 July 1914, her Hungarian nationality and pan-Europeanism made her agonisingly aware that the British Government was not 'giving enough attention to the assassination of Archduke Franz Ferdinand'; she warned Lloyd George at a breakfast meeting that war in Serbia would lead to a European-wide conflagration.[3] Dismissed as 'alarmist', all she could do was wait for her prophetic words to come true.

In the frenetic days before war broke out, the strength and international depth of the women's movement was visible. By some strange coincidence, as well as Rosika, IWSA members from Germany, France, Italy, Holland, Canada and America were in or passing through London. Others cabled heartfelt pleas for peace or mediation, including German leader Frida Perlen from Stuttgart, 'Is it possible the Alliance arranges immediately manifestations for peace?'[4]

Nineteen days after meeting Lloyd George, Rosika had convinced British IWSA members that a personal last-ditch appeal should be made in letters to the many ambassadors in London, pleading with them to exert influence over their respective governments to avert war. With an undercurrent suffrage message, the letters pointed out that, 'The fate of Europe depends on decisions which women have no power to shape.'[5] Although Millicent felt posting these 'with a penny stamp' would be as effective as hand delivering them, she appeared out-manoeuvred. Hailing a London cab, she, Rosika and Crystal Macmillan set about hand delivering this 'Mediation Appeal' on behalf of 12 million suffragists across twenty-six countries. Stopping first at the British Foreign Office, Millicent placed the letter in a footman's hands, requesting he deliver it. Insisting the other two remain in the taxi, she repeated this performance at every embassy – Rosika never forgave her for not personally delivering the letters. It is unlikely that whether placed in a footman's or ambassador's hands, the appeal would have made any difference but the anecdote shows countless suffragists' desperation to avert war and points to conflicts to come.

Other suffrage organisations were also striving for peace. A Women's Rally for Peace was proposed for 8 p.m. on 4 August to urge neutrality on the British Government and mediation between Austro-Hungary and Serbia. Using well-oiled suffrage machinery, a hall was booked, leaflets printed, articles inserted in newspapers, speakers contacted. To demonstrate women's solidarity, Rosika proposed to the organising committee that anti-suffragists Mary Ward and Violet Markham as well as the militant Pankhursts be invited to speak. Her suggestion fell on largely deaf ears. Nevertheless, apart from the WSPU, most other suffrage groups were well represented to hear Millicent, the meeting's president, declare 'war was insensate devilry' – although she announced that despite still being disenfranchised, women 'as citizens now have our duty to perform'.[6] Over 2,000 women crowded inside, hundreds were turned away. By the time this 'last rally of peace forces and common sense' ended at 10 p.m. and a deputation of women took the resolutions to Downing Street, a declaration of war was but an hour away.[7]

Time would soon demonstrate how differently women would interpret Millicent's call to 'duty'. She herself saw this as accepting that 'women's freedom was indefinitely postponed and that this was the supreme sacrifice demanded of us at this stupendous moment'.[8] For some women, many sacrifices included the tight friendships and support networks forged in the depths of the suffrage campaign as, from the moment war was declared, even women on the Kingsway Hall platform found themselves on opposing sides of the peace 'divide'.

Within days, Millicent advised women 'Your country needs you'.[9] On 8 September 1914, Christabel Pankhurst, newly returned from the 'safe' house in France from where she had directed WSPU militancy and avoided arrest, spoke to adoring supporters at an Allied flag-bedecked London Opera House on 'THE GREAT NEED OF VIGOROUS NATIONAL DEFENCE AGAINST THE GERMAN PERIL'. She herself 'hoped to do something to rouse the spirit of militancy in men'.[10] In November, *Jus Suffragii* (the IWSA international journal) editor Mary Sheepshanks pleaded with women across all nations to 'devote [themselves] to putting a stop to such wickedness for ever'. The breach between many suffragists was becoming unbridgeable.

Peace did not reign in the British suffrage camp. Stung by pro-suffrage Lord Robert Cecil's 'great regret' about the August Peace Rally, in February 1915 Millicent wanted the NUWSS to throw its weight behind the war effort.[11] Although she conceded that individuals might go to the proposed Women's Congress at The Hague, she ordered NUWSS societies not to consider themselves free to appoint delegates.[12]

## The Women's Congress at The Hague: a 'pow-wow with the fraus'.

Mary Sheepshanks's plea had born fruit. Holding the 1915 Congress in Berlin being impossible, on 1 December 1914, Dutch suffragist leader Dr

*Right:* Millicent Fawcett.
(*Own collection*)

*Below:* Charlotte Despard outside Downing Street before the war.

Members of the Tax Resistance League.

Anti-suffrage postcard.
(http://womansuffragememorabilia.com)

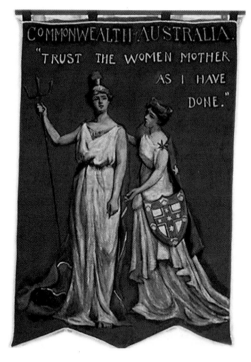

Anti-suffrage postcard.
(http://womansuffragememorabilia.com)

Australia banner suffrage procession, 1908.

Mary Allen (right) and Margaret Damer
Dawson. (Wiki)

Constance Markievicz. (Irish Times)

Prison matron, (l to
r) Hettie, Winnie
and Alice Wheeldon
in Derby prison,
January 1917.

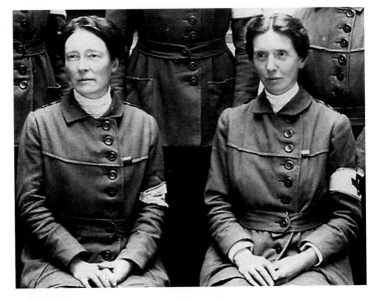

Louisa Garrett Anderson and Flora Murray (WSPU badges visible on their left side). (http://www.ncbi.nim.nih.gov/pmc/tools/openftlist/)

Edith Chaplin, Lady Londonerry. (bbc.co.uk)

Helen Gwynne-Vaugham. (Portrait by William Orpen)

Mona Chalmers Watson. (Portrait by William Orpen)

Mary Ward and her daughter Dorothy. (Wiki commens)

Violet Markham. (http://www/deedsnotwordstowardsliberation.com/100–derbyshire-women-1?lightbox=dataItem-iqjwune11)

Gertrude Bell.
(Gazette Live)

Sylvia Pankhurst.
(Feminist fightback)

Charlotte Despard.
(NPG)

Maude Royden. (http://hdl.handle.
net/2440/90907)

Lena Ashwell. (Author's collection)

Emily Hobhouse.
(theheritageportal)

Evelina Haverfield (L) and Emmeline Pankhurst in court. 2015 Serbian Stamp depicting Evelina Haverfield. (wikicommons, stamp: author's collection)

Kathleen Burke with General Nivelle, New York Times, 24th December 1916.

Mary Borden. (awm.gov)

Aletta Jacobs offered neutral Holland as host. In a letter circulated to the twenty-six IWSA suffrage societies, *Jus* proposed delegates should 'discuss the principles on which peace should be made and … act internationally'. Deep divisions within (not only) the various British suffrage societies soon occurred with a spate of resignations from prominent positions, many suffragists followed Millicent in seeing 'it akin to treason to talk of peace'.[13] *The Suffragette*, mouthpiece for Emmeline and Christabel Pankhurst's WSPU, was not alone in its vocal opprobrium. Sylvia Pankhurst remembered, 'The Press condemned it; prominent women assailed it. We who had agreed to go were execrated'.[14] The 180 British women from across the suffrage spectrum who applied to attend the Women's International Congress at The Hague included Sylvia Pankhurst, Charlotte Despard, Maude Royden and Emily Hobhouse.

Now a bureaucratic obstacle was erected, namely passports, introduced in 1914 to enable the authorities to control all foreign travel. Spurred on by anti-suffragist Lady Jersey, the government announced it was refusing 'permits to delegates'.[15] One delegate, Catherine Marshall, had sufficient influence over Home Secretary Reginald McKenna to persuade him to issue passports to twenty-four women of his choice. This seemed better than nothing. Crystal Macmillan and Kathleen Courtney left immediately to assist with the organisation which, across a war-torn continent, proved a gargantuan task (suffrage machinery was soon in action again).

The British press roared in fury, using terms such as 'Cranquettes' and 'Peacettes'. In language reminiscent of the militancy campaigns, the *Daily Express* referred to would-be attendees as 'sorrowful spinsters'. American delegates, whose ship was halted in the English Channel because, mysteriously, all traffic had been stopped, suffered similar treatment. 'Folly in Petticoats' trumpeted *Sunday Pictorial*; in *The Globe* (9 April 1915), spy novelist William Le Quex excoriated this 'shipload of hysterical women', siding with Mrs Pankhurst who 'has publicly disclaimed all connection with this movement and lamented that her daughter [Sylvia] "should be associated with it"'.

With the American contingent at sea, their twenty-four British counterparts were equally frustrated. At Tilbury, from whence the women were due to sail, a genial McKenna handed out the passports, then announced that regrettably, by Order of the Admiralty, the North Sea was closed to all shipping. And closed it remained; British delegates could only gaze disconsolately out to sea as the Congress unfolded in The Hague. On 27 April 1915 *News From Everywhere*, gleefully reported that 'All Tilbury is laughing at the Peacettes, misguided Englishwomen, who, baggage in hand, are waiting for a boat to take them to Holland where they are anxious to talk peace with German frau over the teapot'. Staging a 'sit-in', the Peacettes remained in Tilbury until the Congress closed.

The British Government had allowed the Americans to sail at the very last minute. Two of their delegates, Jane Addams and Emily Blach, both subsequently won a Nobel Peace Prize. Swedish, Norwegian, German, Hungarian, Italian, Belgian, Austrian, Canadian, Danish, and Dutch delegates attended packed sessions extending over the four days (French and Russian governments were more successful than the British at banning all attendees). When the twenty-eight German delegates returned home, they were arrested.[16] Two schools of thought emerged: those who wanted to stop the war immediately and those who wanted to stop it happening again. By the final day, seven resolutions had been hammered out as well as one stating actions to be taken immediately after the congress, women from neutral countries visited Ambassadors with their proposals.[17] American President Wilson later told Jane Addams that they were the best plans of any put forward; his 1919 Fourteen Points closely resemble the suffragists' solutions for conflict resolution.

In the short-term, the Congress did not achieve its aim of settling the war. Its great significance was that it happened at all. Despite vituperation, bellicosity and ridicule, the much-scorned 'chirruping' suffrage women had meticulously organised an international gathering at a time when European nations were hell-bent on destroying each other. Despite ongoing 'shuttle diplomacy' with women delegates seeking interviews with statesmen in fourteen capitals, the Congress's lasting legacy was the creation of the Women's International League for Peace and Freedom (WILPF) which operates to this day, still striving to bring peace to a war-wracked world.

## Sylvia Pankhurst (1882–1960) 'the pluckiest girl I ever knew'.

In the summer of 1915, addressing Sylvia Pankhurst, Home Secretary Reginald McKenna, creator of the 'Cat and Mouse' Act, begged to shake 'hands with … the pluckiest girl I ever knew'.[18] Despite the depths of antagonism between McKenna and the suffragettes, and his attempted obstruction of the Women's Congress, there is no hint that he was speaking ironically.

Sylvia was Emmeline Pankhurst's second, never greatly beloved, daughter. From an early age, Sylvia recognised that Christabel was their mother's favourite, she and another sister Adela trailed behind. Almost from the moment of birth, socialist and feminist politics were in the very air the Pankhurst offspring breathed. As demands for women's political enfranchisement intensified, Sylvia threw her weight and multiple talents into the struggle. A gifted artist who had gained one of the Royal College of Art's rare women's scholarships, she created much of the WSPU's artwork. Hinting at her future joint commitment not only to universal female suffrage but also to working women whose lives she would strive to ameliorate and which was a key factor in the 1913 Pankhurst family split which by the end of the war was irrevocable, her design for the WSPU membership card portrayed working women in clogs, aprons and shawls.

To Emmeline (and Christabel), who on 10 August 1914 had ordered the cessation of all hostile suffrage acts and total dedication to the War Effort, Sylvia's emerging pacifism and her continued demand for female enfranchisement were incomprehensible. When, at the 8 September 1914 Opera House rally, a male supporter cried out 'Votes for Women', to Sylvia's dismay, Christabel replied, 'We cannot discuss that now'.[19] Sylvia had suffered numerous hunger, thirst and sleep strikes, frequently released from prison more dead than alive, often being carried to subsequent suffrage meetings on a stretcher, with tough East Enders, amongst whom she now lived, endeavouring to create a human shield around her to prevent her being rearrested and returned to prison. Christabel seemed to have abandoned the cause for which hundreds of women including those from the working class but not she herself who directed the campaign from France, had sacrificed their health and risked their livelihoods.

Pankhurst family tensions had initially surfaced over Emmeline's autocratic leadership and WSPU's policies and what Sylvia considered their jettisoning of working-class women in favour of the more socially privileged; she saw female enfranchisement as one aspect of social improvement rather than a goal in and of itself. Christabel had vociferously criticised Sylvia's belief that working-class women should be deeply involved in the struggle, 'working women were the weakest portion of the sex ... We want picked women, the very strongest and most intelligent!' Unknowingly echoing anti-suffragist Gertrude Bell, Christabel claimed, 'their education [was] too meagre to equip them for the contest'.[20]

So out of tune were Sylvia's ideas that she formed the militant East London Federation of Suffragettes (ELF), initially affiliated to the WSPU but subsequently ousted from the mother organisation. She campaigned for Keir Hardie and the wider Labour Party (formerly supported and now ditched by the WSPU). Despite espousing militancy, Sylvia felt that this should be directed less towards attacks on property and more towards a 'mass struggle'.[21] Between the ELF's inception in February 1913 and August 1914, Sylvia was arrested eight times; she also organised rent strikes, a stratagem she encouraged during the war, and became ever more closely involved in, and supportive of, socialist politics.

Sylvia edited the ELF's paper, *Women's Dreadnought* (changed during the war to *Workers' Dreadnought*), launched to coincide with and give coverage to a working-class suffragette demonstration in Trafalgar Square on 8 March 1914, International Women's Day. Five men and five women including Sylvia were subsequently arrested and charged; demonstrators were male and female and their social backgrounds chimed with the ELF's direction of travel. Throughout the war, Sylvia used the paper to give working women a voice. It also became a powerful pacifist organ which, unlike the mainstream press, tried to report accurately on pacifist activities.

With two Pankhursts rallying their troops and vociferously encouraging men to enlist, Sylvia was fighting a different campaign. Whilst not dropping her demands for the vote, she strove to draw attention to the multiple hardships facing women living in the East End – of which she was intimately aware, having long lived in the area. Food prices spiralled immediately. In a 6 August 1914 letter to the *Daily Mail*, NUWSS Lady Frances Balfour stated, 'Let there be no complaining in our streets ... women can save the situation by accepting it ... Such people should be treated as deserters.' Sylvia begged to differ. On 24 August, *Daily Herald* reported on a 'splendid meeting held at Poplar Dock Gates', it was 'demanded that the government should take immediate control of the food supply so all may feed or starve together without regard to wealth or social position and that working women should be consulted in the fixing of prices and the distribution of food'.

The food situation was becoming so desperate that Sylvia was appealing for donations of milk to feed starving babies. Many suffragettes sent money, and a milk distribution centre was set up to assist the neediest infants. Another initiative was a cost price restaurant – again she appealed for funds so that a meal could be provided at 2*d* per adult and a 1*d* per child, with a cup of tea costing a farthing (¼*d*). 'Free meals will be given in urgently necessitous cases'. *The Times* (29 September 1914) printed the ELF's appeal for funds. This restaurant continued throughout the war.

It may seem puzzling that in a country that prided itself on being civilised and where separation allowances were paid to soldiers' dependents (partly funded out of the soldier's own pay), countless soldiers' wives were not only dependent on heavily subsidised restaurants or milk banks to feed themselves and their children but, unable to pay their rent, were constantly threatened with eviction. By November, the evictions of Glaswegian soldiers' wives reached scandalous proportions with 500 summonses for non-payment issued a week. Separation Allowances, when these were paid (often weeks in arrears), were totally inadequate, starting at 1*s* 1*d* a day for a private's wife rising to 2*s* 3*d* for a Warrant Officer's; 2*d* a day was paid for each child. In 1914, 3½lb cheese cost 2*s* 4*d*, 215 per cent of Mrs Tommy Atkins's daily separation allowance. In 1917, when allowances had barely increased, the cost of a 4lb loaf of bread had more than doubled from 5½*d* to 1*s*.

To make matters worse, the Soldiers' and Sailors' Families Association officials saw the allowances as 'charitable acts or grace not an entitled allowance'.[22] Middle-class do-gooders descended upon working-class areas to establish a soldier's wife's morality and thus whether she was, in their minds, entitled to the allowance that was being deducted from her husband's pay. In Newcastle, wives were given food tickets as opposed to money and could only purchase items from an approved list.[23] A West Ham alderman told the press in November 1914, 'I don't believe that one woman in 20 is receiving the full amount she is entitled to from the War Office'.[24] The situation, graphically described in *The Home Front*, spurred Sylvia on to ever greater efforts on behalf of the voiceless women amongst whom she lived and reinforced both her socialist and pacifist principles. On 14 November 1914, *Herald* advertised a public meeting at Caxton Hall, Westminster, scene of so many suffrage meetings: 'Stand Up for the Soldier's Wife'. Its purpose: to 'protest against the government's attempts to insult the

Soldier's Wife by threatening her with Police Supervision, the stoppage of her allowance, exclusion from the public house and other restrictions on the liberty of women'. Speakers included 'a soldier's wife' and Sylvia Pankhurst. Committed suffragist Evelyn Sharp (who in 1915 began writing for *Herald*) took the Chair.

Outraged by hearing that soldiers' wives had to help to kit out their men, often ending up in debt to supply the barest essentials (in his memoirs Asquith conceded that Lord Kitchener had admitted 'the recruits had been badly treated in the way of clothing, books and other necessaries'), Sylvia arranged a meeting with Kitchener's deputy, Harold Baker. She hoped the plain-speaking East End wives might convince him of the iniquities visited upon them and their soldier husbands. He informed her, 'I do not want to listen to actual cases … I only want to hear officials.'[25] Used to such rebuffs, Sylvia doubled her efforts on behalf of these downtrodden women. She sent copies of *Woman's Dreadnought* to local dignitaries and local Committee representatives. As hard-hitting during the war as it had been from its inception, there was a distinct feeling amongst many readers that in this paper at least 'you get the truth'.

Equal pay would soon be added to Sylvia's multiple campaigns. In the war's early days, thousands of men and women had been thrown out of work. Sylvia believed that 'the State was leaving unemployment and hardship to do the work of raising a 'volunteer army as men who were physically fit' were denied unemployment dole or other financial assistance.[26] To try to ease distress amongst unemployed women or indeed soldiers' wives, the NUWSS set up employment and training bureaus; to Sylvia's fury these offered little more than 'sweated' wages. Similarly, the Queen's Work For Women Fund, established 20 August 1914 in collaboration with women's labour leader Mary MacArthur, speedily, 'covered itself in ignominy, by setting up the sweated wages of 10 shillings/week'.[27] Sylvia wrote to Queen Mary challenging these rates of pay. Attempting to counter the sweated wages, the ELF established its own workshops paying 5*d* per hour or £1 per week for weekly paid workers. Hearing that £1 was being paid, the future MP Nancy Astor informed Sylvia that had she known of this high rate of pay, she would not have supported the enterprise; discovering that Sylvia intended to go to The Hague, she again rebuked her.[28] The 21 November 1914 *Herald* commended Sylvia's enterprises which were nevertheless 'hampered through lack of capital' and listed readers who had sent financial contributions. Sylvia never abandoned her campaigns, her December 1916 Caxton Hall 'Sweated Industries Exhibition' drew attention to both women's appalling pay and their 'ridiculously inadequate separation allowances'.[29]

As the demand for women workers increased, Sylva stepped up her demands for equal pay. *Woman's Dreadnought* (20 March 1915) highlighted how 'To the women whom they have refused to grant the rights of enfranchised citizens, the Government through the President of the Board of Trade has issued an appeal to enlist for War Service'. She continues, 'it is absolutely imperative that *women who are to be enlisted as recruits in the National War Service shall have the Vote at once.'* Had Emmeline Pankhurst, who would soon be organising the women's 'Right to Serve' rally on behalf of the government made female enfranchisement a condition of her involvement, might a desperate government have acceded to her demands?

Like other pacifist suffragists, Sylvia was involved with the No-Conscription Fellowship. When conscription (which Sylvia knew would place undue burdens on working-class women) was mooted, the ELF had lobbied Parliament hoping (perhaps naively) they could persuade MPs to vote against the bill. On 8 April 1916, a huge demonstration took place at Trafalgar Square. Its 'focus was to oppose the full scope of the government's repressive legislation.'[30] About 20,000 attended with Sylvia sharing a platform with inter alia Charlotte Despard and Eva Gore-Booth. The women were physically and verbally abused, largely by 'colonial troops who had been organised to disrupt the meeting.'[31] When Emmeline, in America rallying support for the Allies, read the newspaper reports, her cabled outrage was broadcast on the radio, further alienating mainstream suffrage support for Sylvia. The nurseries and milk centres, so heavily dependent upon suffrage donations, experienced a significant drop in income.

Meanwhile even ELF members who had initially supported a 'just' war were having doubts. Women who had previously held rallies demanding the Vote were now holding Peace demonstrations at the East London Docks and Victoria Park. *Workers' Dreadnought* became a key organ for providing information about peace campaigns, further distancing Sylvia from Emmeline and Christabel. Parenthetically, it was *Workers' Dreadnought* that first published Siegfried Sassoon's famous July 1917 protest 'Finished With War: A Soldier's Declaration'.

A late December 1916 rally at the East India Dock Gates led to several arrests, 'rescues' according to the *Nottingham Evening Post*, to protect speakers, including a then unknown Clement Atlee, and Sylvia from hostile crowds.[32] It is hard to see these as rescues – multiple papers report that the detained were all charged with obstruction and other offences and fined £2 (£160 today) or seven days imprisonment. Sylvia turned the tables and stated police interference had caused the trouble.

The authorities would soon have greater reason to watch Sylvia. Not this time for her suffrage or pacifist activities although she was speaking across the land demanding the removal of the age bar for women voters and organising and speaking at peace rallies, but for her vocal and journalistic support of the Russian Revolution. Whilst globe-trotting Emmeline officially visited Russia to rally support for the Tsar, Sylvia was applauding the Bolsheviks, demanding a 'League of Rights' for soldiers and sailors. With the benefit of hindsight, it is hard to understand the rose-tinted spectacles through which Sylvia viewed the Bolsheviks but view them so she did, becoming involved in the 'Hands Off Russia' campaign and subsequently visiting Lenin. She, fellow pacifist Charlotte Despard with whom she sometimes shared a platform, and countless others were placed under police surveillance and a 'Weekly Intelligence Summary' was sent, ironically to Charlotte's brother Sir John French. The contrast between these women's views and those of the 'sound' Pankhursts was ever more pronounced. With 'Lloyd George's approval, a group of business magnates had given Christabel £15,000 (over £1 million today) for her anti–socialist campaigning'.[33]

Less than euphoric about the Representation of the People Act, in October 1918 Sylvia continued to goad the authorities. Charged with causing 'sedition amongst the forces or the civil population' for which she conducted her own defence, she was fined £50 (£3,100 today) with £8 5s (£540) costs. She had stated, and would continue to state long after the guns fell silent, that 'the war was not a war of freedom or liberation but a sordid scramble between two groups of capitalists.'[34] With the London Police having recently struck, her warning 'that when you have a police strike, you are not far from a soldiers' strike' would have made grim reading for politicians who knew that winning the peace would be as hard as winning the war. Sylvia would remain a thorn in the government's side.

'Plucky' to the end, for Sylvia the decades after the Armistice were as turbulent as those which preceded it. In the 1930s, she took up the struggle against fascism and also for a country that would mark the remaining three decades of her life, Ethiopia, where she died in 1960. Buried in a special plot reserved for Ethiopia's heroes, a memorial service was held for her in 1961 in London's Caxton Hall, scene of so many of her suffrage and pacifist speeches and battles.

## Charlotte Despard (1844–1939): 'the supreme form of courage which does not falter in the face of overwhelming opposition'.[35]

The government's refusal to issue Charlotte Despard with a passport to attend The Hague Congress did not surprise her. Her long campaigning as a Poor Law guardian and a spokesman for East Enders, and her commitment to suffragism which had landed her in prison, had not endeared her to the Establishment. With her brother Field Marshall Sir John French commanding the British Expeditionary Force, on paper, she seems an unlikely 'peacette'. Yet, already showing the shape of things to come, fifteen years earlier she had spoken out against the Boer War, the self-same war that had earned John his knighthood.

Charlotte's path to suffragism stemmed largely from her work with the poorest of London's poor. Born to affluence and privilege, after being widowed in 1890, she became involved with Nine Elms, Battersea, then a slum area. But rather than descend on the 'poor' as a Lady Bountiful, she dedicated herself to the area. Using her inheritance, she set up a health clinic, a soup kitchen for the local unemployed and clubs for both working men and youths and converted to Roman Catholicism. Along with the religion, she discarded the elaborate costumes of her social class, favouring simple clothes, open-toed sandals and her hallmark black lace mantilla. During the week, she lived above one of her welfare 'shops'. Elected to Lambeth's Poor Law Board in 1894, to many Guardians' displeasure, she began exposing corruption and mismanagement, willful or otherwise. Soon a committed socialist, 'She proved herself a brilliant committee woman, bringing a rare combination of informed compassion, practical experience, and military efficiency to the board's deliberations.'[36]

Sir John was not unsupportive of Charlotte's endeavours. He accepted her periodically invading the 'peace and quietness' of the Surrey home she had lent him when she turned up with a busload of Battersea's poor, complete with 'barrel-organs'; he proved adept at organising 'sports for the men'.[37] When she gave her first speech as a Poor Law member, he assured her 'Only nervous people are ever of real use.'[38] Public speaking and suffragism would soon hold no fears.

Her work at Lambeth made her deeply conscious that, 'turn which way I would, I knocked my head against laws to which neither I nor my sisters had consented and which we were bound to obey'.[39] Unable to change these laws which did not strike her as drafted by 'the most enlightened of men', she joined the Adult Suffrage League (this commitment to universal suffrage would eventually lead her to clash with Emmeline Pankhurst). By the summer of 1906, Charlotte was honorary secretary of the WSPU and in February 1907 she managed to get arrested. With brother John now tipped as the next Inspector General of the Armed Forces, the police had been warned against detaining her. Aware that in her mantilla and sandals she was highly visible, she successfully 'donned a motoring hat with a streaming veil'.[40] Sentenced to twenty-one days, with her sparse lifestyle, the prison regime bothered her not at all. Writing in 1908 about her commitment to suffragism, Charlotte felt that despite her great campaigns for social justice (which she waged for the rest of her life), 'I had not found what I met on the threshold of this young, vigorous Union of Hearts'.[41] Suffragism would lead her into stormy waters.

During a second imprisonment in 1909, by which time she had broken with the WSPU, a fellow prisoner noted 'a command[ing] figure ... looking, if possible, more dignified than ever, in the quaint uniform of the criminal'.[42] Never one to waste an opportunity, having made great capital of her 'snowy hair' at her trial, Charlotte subsequently used her personal prison experiences to draw attention to the plight of those female prisoners whose incarceration, unlike her own, was not considered politically sensitive. Released early, the authorities expressed concern for her apparent ill-health which she disputed, 'my health was perfectly good'. She was elected president of the Women's Freedom League (WFL), formed after a split with the WSPU over Emmeline's autocratic leadership, and whose first year's expenses she underwrote. Styling themselves 'constitutionalist militants', the WFL also encouraged passive (including tax) resistance. She was behind women's refusal to supply information to the April 1911 censors.[43] Despite many suffrage societies now accepting that limited female enfranchisement would be a step in the right direction, she remained committed to universal adult suffrage and spoke passionately on multiple platforms. As a speaker she met with opprobrium, some violence and deep admiration. By then in her late 60s, she was prominent in pageants and marches and, with black mantilla fluttering, invariably led the WFL contingent.

By the time she attended the lavish IWSA 1913 Budapest Congress, 'Granny Despard' was a key figure, not only in the suffrage movement and for her slum work but also, like Mary Ward, for her concerns for disabled children. The welcome she received from the 3,000 Budapest delegates was only surpassed by that given to the IWSA's America President.[44]

Having spoken at the Kingsway Peace Rally, Charlotte's relief committees reinstated her in her family's eyes in the war's very early days. Relations who had 'locked up their daughters for fear that Aunt Lottie would take them on political sprees that would land them in Holloway' enthusiastically joined in; her suffrage sister Katherine Harley went with her two adult daughters to run a hospital Unit in Serbia where Katherine was killed in late 1916.[45] However, Charlotte never attended recruitment campaigns to drum up volunteers for the army, of which brother John was now commander-in-chief. Nor did she ever consider Germans 'Teuton fiends'. Despite sharing her friends' and her brother's admiration for 'our splendid men', her pacifist colours became apparent when she helped organise and attempted to attend The Hague Congress, subsequently joining the WIL. She declared herself a pacifist 'in the sense that all women should be pacifists. Their fight should not be with weapons of war, but with spiritual darkness in high places.'[46]

In late September 1915, just as the British Army was engaged at Loos in its largest (most disastrous) conflict to date which shredded Sir John's reputation, Charlotte was addressing a crowd of thousands at Trafalgar Square. She was no stranger to this venue, it was the scene of her and Nina Boyle's arrest in 1913 and she had also spoken at the enormous 2 August 1914 peace rally. This time, speaking against conscription, she shared a platform with, amongst others, Sylvia Pankhurst. Like Sylvia, the treatment meted out to soldiers' wives deeply concerned her and they buried earlier differences to try to ease the mounting distress in the East End. Linking her philanthropic endeavours to her beliefs, aid was carried out through the WFL's National Aid Corps. Alongside working for mothers, destitute children and the near-starving, she set up workshops to offer employment, and a fifty-bed hospital – which she funded. She initiated attempts to help those considered 'enemy aliens', whom she felt women suffragists should help as they had received such generous hospitality abroad. More controversial were her anti-war public speaking engagements, but, like many older pacifists steeled by their suffrage-platform days, hostile crowds bothered her not at all.

In 1917, 73-year-old Charlotte joined the Committee of the Women's Peace Crusade, described as the first truly popular campaign linking feminism and anti-militarism which aimed to stop the war by negotiation.[47] Another exhausting country-wide speaking tour ensued. Like many suffragists, she hailed the 1917 Russian Revolution as a triumph for democracy and women's suffrage. At the June 1917 Labour Socialist and Democratic Convention, she seconded a resolution calling on the government 'to place itself in accord with the democracy of Russia.' The convention was won over by her oratorical powers undiminished by increasing years.

Charlotte's rejoicing at the passing of the January 1918 Representation of the People Act was muted. Her goal of universal adult suffrage had not been achieved. She stood as the Labour candidate in the 1918 elections and although defeated, polled a sizable number of votes for a 74-year-old woman who had spent the last two decades flying in the face of public opinion. Had all wards resembled Nine Elms, she would have been a shoo-in.

Having resigned the presidency of the WFL, Charlotte attended the May 1919 Women's International Congress in Zurich. Like so many British delegates she was horrified at the emaciated state of women from defeated countries, many of whom were so close to starvation that they could not eat the Congress food. The war might have been over but the long road back to some semblance of normality had hardly begun. For Charlotte herself, now living in Ireland, new campaigns (against British rule in Ireland, and against Fascism) soon beckoned.

## Maude Royden (1876–1956) 'War was the woman's worst enemy'.

The many attendees at the June 1913 Budapest Congress included Maude Royden, who felt bemused by many international women's expectation of a future European war. The youngest, slightly disabled, daughter of a wealthy Tory MP, Maude had studied History at Lady Margaret Hall, Oxford. After eighteen months working at Liverpool's Victoria Women's Settlement where a clergyman, Hudson Shaw, spotted her oratorical abilities, she returned to Oxford in 1905 becoming the first female lecturer for the Oxford University Extension scheme, initially listed only by her initials to mask her gender. She joined the NUWSS in 1908. Rapidly rising through their ranks, she became an Executive Committee member in 1911, editor of *Common Cause* in 1913. (She resigned both the editorship and her membership in 1915 due to the NUWSS's stance towards The Hague Congress.[48]) Her 'magnetic public speaking was renowned' and she gave 'classes to tyro speakers'.[49] Based in London by 1912, she had addressed 267 suffrage meetings.[50] However, she refused an invitation to debate with Gladys Pott which she later regretted.

In 1913 Maude's speaking skills were such that the Bishop of Winchester asked her to address 2,000 men at a church congress on the then hot topic of 'Social Purity'. Many suffrage supporters were outraged by contemporary double sexual standards (latterly one of Christabel Pankhurst's main platforms). Maude's Christian feminism was based on Christ's rather than St Paul's teachings about women; for her, the constitutional women's movement was a deeply moral one, not all clergymen agreed. Speaking out forcefully against suffragette militancy, she was a member of multiple suffrage societies, she helped found and became chairman of the Church League for Women's Suffrage (CLWS).

Despite finding war abhorrent, Maude's road to pacifism was fraught, eventually coming to believe that international women should come together to declare a 'war against war' and prepare for peace. As a member of the British organising Committee, Maude intended to attend the 1915 Hague Congress. Then, on 7 April, ASL Vice President Lady Jersey, 'well accustomed to giving a guiding hand to politicians' (she had no need of the vote as she exerted significant political influence behind the scenes), wrote a long letter to the Home Office advising that the women be prevented from attending the Congress. She singled out the 'very eloquent' Maude as 'exactly the sort of women who would make a moving address … to our injury in neutral countries'.[51]

Barred from attending, Maude received briefings from The Hague, she was invited to become a Vice-chair of the WIL and continued to speak about peace and the women's movement. In *Herald* (8 May 1915) she discussed how women, upon whom 'the statesmanship of the world has brought the indescribable horrors of the war' and women who were trying to discuss how '*in future* such horrors might be avoided', were being silenced. So silenced that telephones were tapped and letters from abroad not delivered.[52] No doubt to Lady Jersey's horror, and in a manner reminiscent of the NUWSS 1913 Pilgrimage at which she had been a moving speaker, Maude joined a caravan crusade intent on taking a message of Christian Pacifism to the country. With the recent sinking of the *Lusitania*, the first aerial bombardments and the never-ending casualty lists, they were swimming against the tide of public opinion. Accusations of being spies were hurled at crusaders. In Leicestershire in July 1915, things came to an ugly head, everything was burned and, set upon by a mob of 2–3,000 which the police were unable to control, the pacifists finally admitted defeat. Even Maude conceded, 'to go on preaching peace to people in such straits … seemed intolerable'.[53]

Shaken by the ugly scenes she had witnessed, although Maude continued to work for the WIL, she now directed her energies away from outright pacifism and towards a different, equally controversial, goal. Having been a keynote speaker at a campaign to seek female participation in the Councils of the Church, she was soon in direct conflict with the highest ecclesiastical authorities in the land.[54] In 1915, a bereaved mother, Mrs Parker had poured scorn on the 'oil of comfort' which 'tender men of God' tried to offer her in her grief for her son.[55] Men, Mrs Parker concluded, could not understand a mother's grief. Maude, who squirmed when vicars told bereaved women that 'they knew what they were going through', would have agreed. Might a woman do better?

Maude was becoming either nationally famous (or notorious) and not only for her suffragism and pacifism. She was arguing that women (who could be ordained in Non-Conformist sects) should also be ordained into the Church of England; in 1916, she published a pamphlet accordingly. Despite these almost heretical views, the established church realised it could use her talents in its 1916 'National Mission of Repentance and Hope', which, using lay female and ordained male 'missionaries', aimed to re-Christianise the war-traumatised land.[56] A future Archbishop of Canterbury appointed her to the Mission Council. Bishops then worried about where the women, who were banned from pulpits, were to speak. Eventually, Maude and her sister preachers were given episcopal dispensation to deliver their message … from the foot of the chancel steps, but only women and children could listen.[57] One friend noted that anti-militancy suffragist Maude was becoming an 'ecclesiastical militant'.[58]

Worse followed. In March 1917, Anglican Maude arguing that this would further the women's cause, accepted the post of Assistant Preacher at the non-conformist City Temple in London.[59] Several newspapers greeted her appointment ambiguously, suggesting 'she would have preferred St Paul's Cathedral but City Temple is not such a poor second best'.[60] One, snidely referring to Maude's pacifism and championing of the Labour Party, noted how her shipping-magnate father's firm 'had invested an enormous sum in the latest War Loan'. 'If Miss Royden followed her father in politics and religion, she would be a firm adherent of Conservatism and the Church of England' (and doubtless an anti-suffragist and war-monger as well).[61] The Roydens were another family divided by politics and war. Irrespective of her seeming apostasies, Maude regularly filled the enormous Temple to capacity.

When the partial franchise finally became law, Maude preached at the City Temple's Service of Thanksgiving. Was she behind the choice of the hymn which included the line 'And every vote be cast for Thee'?[62] Deftly changing the language of a verse from Ecclesiastes to, 'Let us now praise famous women and the mothers who begat them', Maude the Suffragist, Maude the Pacifist's sermon intertwined these beliefs, she reminded worshippers that suffragists had 'laid down their weapons' but still achieved their goal.[63] Thanksgiving services were widely held with Maude in great demand to preach. More surprising was the address pacifist Maude gave at City Temple's 'Women's Parade'. She assured the massed ranks of women engaged in military service, 'Your Country is Proud of You' and begged them not to forget 'what we went to war for, the ideals on which depend the future of the world'.[64] If the text of this sermon was uncontroversial and to some newspapers she might now be 'one of the most distinguished women of the age', she was not afraid to publish her views on the state of the world. Thus, on Easter Sunday 1918, 'Many of us feel … that millions of precious lives have been thrown away, not for the sake of righteousness but to cover up the blunders of paralyzed statesmen … unwilling or unable to direct the storm they have unleashed.'[65]

The biggest controversies with the Anglican authorities were still to come. In September 1918, Hudson Shaw invited Maude to preach at St Botolph's

Bishopsgate; on previous occasions she had read the lesson, even this was considered daring. Now, as part of a series of well-publicised Thursday addresses, wearing 'a cassock and surplice [she] dealt eloquently with The League of Nations from the Christian standpoint'; the church was packed.[66] The Bishop of London, Winnington-Ingram, spiritual head of the Armed Forces, publicly rebuked Shaw; he should not start 'another series of Thursday addresses without consulting him.'[67] Undeterred, Shaw arranged that Maude would next preach not on a Thursday, but on Good Friday, the holiest day of the Christian year. Winnington-Ingram erupted, 'I absolutely *forbid* you … to allow Miss Royden to take the Three Hours Service in your church tomorrow'.[68] Shaw 'pasted the prohibition on the door and moved the service to the adjacent parish rooms; those for whom there was no room inside climbed onto window sills to hear Maude castigating the bishops for denying spiritual equality to women in the church'.[69]

With the war over and women's suffrage partially achieved, Maude campaigned to improve mothers' rights and for the League of Nations. Whether speaking or preaching, she drew hundreds. The 17 October 1919 *Surrey Mirror and County Post* advised readers planning to attend a League of Nations meeting at Redhill on 24 October that they had a treat in store for Miss Royden, 'a keen suffragist (not suffragette)' was one of the speakers. 'Full of humour as well as earnestness, she "takes" an audience at once and at a crowded meeting at the Royal Albert Hall [site of so many suffrage rallies], she was the only speaker who had to bow her acknowledgements again and again when her speech was finished.'

For Maude, new challenges lay ahead, the League of Nations would prove ineffective at resolving the crises of the 20s and 30s; it was only in 1994 that the Church of England ordained women priests and, not without controversy, the first woman bishop in 2015. When she began campaigning for women's ordination in 1914, Maude's prediction that women's total integration into the church she loved would take longer to achieve than universal adult suffrage proved prophetic.

## Emily Hobhouse (1860–1926) 'Fearless integrity in the cause of peace'.

When the IWSA proposed platform speakers for the 4 August 1914 Women's Peace Rally, one name which horrified Millicent Fawcett was that of Emily

Hobhouse. The two women had clashed over conditions in the South Africa concentration camps during the Boer War. Emily's actions had damned her in the eyes of many of her compatriots, including 'Imperialist' Millicent's, as a 'traitor'. Although perhaps fortuitously, ill-health prevented her from attending the rally; she urged politicians including Lloyd George, to 'take a bold and noble stand' and keep England out of the war.[70]

In 1899 when the South Africa war began, Emily was already quite well known, less for her non-militant suffragism than for her attempts to improve child labour conditions. Disturbed by the jingoism of the popular press, she joined the South African Conciliation Committee and became honorary secretary of the Women's Branch formed in 1900. Deeply concerned by the effects of Britain's scorched earth policy on Boer women and children, she established and collected money for the South African Women and Children Distress Fund and, in December 1900, went to South Africa to distribute the funds and investigate conditions in the concentration camps established by Britain. Her discoveries horrified her; she returned to England in 1901 and unleashed countless letters to newspapers – the conditions in the concentration camps 'rapidly burgeoned into an international scandal'.[71] The government appointed six women, headed by Millicent Fawcett but excluding Emily, to visit and investigate the camps – Emily considered the ensuing report a whitewash. Nevertheless, she, a mere woman, had made the government take notice of her. It was a lesson she would not forget.

In the years between her return to England and the outbreak of war, Emily became closely involved with the suffrage movement. She was elected Chair of the (1909) People's Suffrage Federation (PSF) which included several high-profile men such as Bertrand Russell, John Galsworthy, historian George Trevelyan (and his wife Janet, Mary Ward's daughter), and Emily's brother Leonard, one of the *Manchester Guardian*'s directors.[72] Their programme of 'one person, one vote' was only achieved in 1948 with the abolition of plural voting.

When war broke out, Emily disagreed with the many women who now believed that 'agitating for peace … was tantamount to treachery', her thoughts turned in a very different direction.[73] At Christmas 1914, using *Jus Suffragii* she sent an 'Open Letter to the Women of Germany and Austria'. Despite 'the Christmas message sound[ing] like mockery to a world at war, those of us who wished and still wish for peace may surely offer a solemn greeting to such of you who feel as we do'. Drawing on her experiences in South Africa, she acknowledged that 'the brunt of modern war falls upon non-combatants, and the conscience of the world cannot bear the sight.' Signed 'in sisterhood of sorrow' by 100 women, the message was one of reconciliation and hope. She urged all women to 'steadily refuse to give credence to those false tales so freely told us, each of the other.'[74] In the New Year, German women responded via *Jus,* reciprocating the British women's greetings.

In late spring 1915, Emily, who had been refused a passport for Holland, travelled to Italy, where she had frequently wintered. With Italy having recently entered the war on the Allies' side, her pacifist leanings were noted by the British Ambassador who complained about her to the Foreign Office. From Italy, she went to neutral Switzerland and, determined to try her hand at peace making, sought an audience with German Ambassador, Gisbert von Romberg. She seemed to believe that Germany would halt submarine activity if 'we would withdraw our Food Blockade'; then to Holland where the Congress had 'unfurled the white flag of peace'. The FO dubbed her a 'peace crank'.[75]

Still determined to pursue the path of peace, by June 1916 Emily had successfully persuaded Ambassador von Romberg to contact German Chancellor Berthmann-Hollweg requesting permission for her to visit Belgium. She intended to report on conditions for civilians and see for herself whether the British press had exaggerated the 'German atrocities'. From Belgium, she proposed progressing to Berlin to report on British civilians held at the great internment camp at Ruhleben. Although the British Ambassador to Switzerland tried to prevent her departure, she was soon en route to Brussels. Accompanied every step of the way by a German Army 'minder' whom she considered 'charming', she spent ten days in Belgium, based at the Astoria Hotel. The prohibition on her interacting with any individual Belgians, about which she expressed regret, successfully concealed the brutality of the Occupation from her. She proclaimed herself sceptical about the well-documented atrocities such as the local population being used as human shields at Charleroi, or the massacre of women and children at Dinant.[76] Furthermore, she naïvely accepted that an accidental fire had burned Louvain.

Leaving for Germany on 17 June, her next coup was to secure an interview in Berlin with German Foreign Minister, Gottlieb von Jagow; they conducted what she described as a 'heart to heart meeting'. She hoped to carry a message of peace from him to the British Foreign Office but admitted that although he was 'good-natured', she had not made much impression on him. She made more impression on fellow IWSA members and the many other internationalist women whom she met. Her final destination was Ruhleben where she stated that the camp commandant 'was known to have done all in his power to make camp life endurable' and listed her fairly positive findings about food, accommodation and 'amusements'.[77]

Convinced that Sir Edward Grey would listen to her, Emily confidently cabled to tell him 'Arrive London about midday await kind instructions Westminster Palace.'[78] Either Grey did not receive the telegram or chose to forget it. When, on 31 October 1916, questions were asked in Parliament relating to her peregrinations, Charles Trevelyan MP pointed out, 'immediately on her return to this country Miss Hobhouse offered to give every possible information she had to the Government', Lord Cecil claimed, 'I did not know anything about that'.[79] More in tune with the country and Parliament's mood was the question posed by Sir John Butch MP, 'Is there no means of bringing to justice a lady who goes abroad for the purpose of betraying her country?' On 24 October 1916, the popular press trumpeted headlines such as 'Whitewashing the Hun' (*Pall Mall Gazette*). Relatively restrained correspondence in *The Times* did little to redeem her or persuade her opponents that however naive her view, her actions were humanitarian and not treasonable.

With the benefit of a century's hindsight, there is no doubt that Emily was driven by pure humanitarianism and a longing to secure peace (she did achieve some exchanges of civilian internees). To the British press, the Establishment, and many of her erstwhile colleagues who never forgave her Boer War report, she was a 'peace crank' who had only seen what she wanted to see. Many suffragists believed that, once again, her interferences harmed the cause. She was intensively interviewed by Basil Thomson, Chief of the Metropolitan Police CID, who found no evidence that she was a spy; he unflatteringly saw her as 'a silly mischievous old woman but not disloyal to the country'.[80] Even many internationalist suffragists rejected her, she was too radical whilst, unforgivably for the constitutionalists, her actions had broken multiple rules.

The government agreed she had broken the rules. One unintended consequence of her peregrinations was that in November 1916, a new regulation was added to DORA, DRR14F: it was illegal for any British subject to enter into enemy (including enemy occupied) territory without the express consent of the Secretary of State.[81]

Perhaps in our more cynical age, it is hard not to feel bemused by Emily Hobhouse's undertakings and belief that she could end the war. Yet whilst countless other women were discussing peace and corresponding with each other via *Jus Suffragii*, she 'was the sole person from any of the warring countries who actually journeyed to the other side in search of peace.'[82] Although she herself would never have put it so crudely, she really had 'tried to stop the bloody thing'.

*Chapter Six*

# At No Cost to the Government

## Taxes, windows and pillar boxes.

Although the cry 'No taxation without representation' is commonly associated with the American colonists who, being unrepresented in the British House of Commons, refused to pay the Stamp Tax, the idea of taxpayer 'representation' dates back to Magna Carta (1215).[1] Constitutional suffragists would have recourse to this ploy and one woman continued this passive protest throughout the war.

Protesting against the Boer War, suffragist Dora Montefiore 'refused willingly to pay income tax, because payment of such tax went towards financing a war in the making of which I had had no voice.' Attracting little publicity, there, 'the matter ended'.[2] In publicity terms, her breakthrough occurred in 1906 when, supported by numerous suffrage groups flying a banner over her house stating, 'Women should vote for the laws they obey and the taxes they pay', Dora awaited the bailiffs' arrival at her London home. The so-called 'Siege of Fort Montefiore' hit numerous newspaper headlines. Sensing publicity potential, in October 1909, Louisa Garrett Anderson invited a group of fellow suffrage supporters including Dora to a meeting at her house. The Tax Resistance League (TRL) was formed. Early members included Lena Ashwell, Charlotte Despard, Evelina Haverfield, and Evelyn Sharp. They agreed that the League should be independent of any suffrage society, flying its own grey and silver banner at subsequent processions.

Many professional women, both militant and constitutionalists, became committed resisters. The League's secretary Margaret Kineton Parkes, an indefatigable public speaker, achieved significant publicity in local newspapers. Her platform was 'women are ruled not by representative Government but tyranny'.[3] Papers reported the numbers of women who refused to pay tax, their imprisonments (some women subsequently went on hunger strike), and their unrepentant statements at sales of their distrained goods which other members often purchased. Anti-suffragists also attended sales. If one Mabel Smith wondered 'what advantages or privilege had men obtained for themselves that were not shared by women?' suffragists begged to believe there were many.[4] Some local newspapers reported sympathetically on the TRL, others less flatteringly; the 11 July 1910 *Globe* considered tax resistance a 'childish expedient'. Childish or not, *Daily Herald* (11 April 1914) estimated that in the year to April 1914, the unrepresented women had paid some £90 million (£945 million today) in Imperial taxes – no estimate is given as to the amount withheld.

On 26 August 1914, most resisters decided to suspend activities due to the National Emergency; Evelyn Sharp disagreed, 'a war fought to save democracy did not seem to me to provide the best reason for supporting the principle of taxation without representation'. On 13 June 1917, the sum she owed reaching £50 (just under £4,000 today), she was handed over to the Bankruptcy Court, where *The Times* noted, she 'declined to give any information about her assets or her calling'. A bailiff arrived and, despite the inauspicious circumstances, over the weeks he spent sitting in her 'best armchair', they became firm friends – she converted him to the Suffrage Cause. When all her possessions had been removed except her clothes and her bed, she missed his 'unobtrusive presence'. She saw the removal of her typewriter, which made it impossible for her to earn her living, as part of a planned 'political persecution'; her letters were also opened during the period she refused to pay what the government deemed she owed. Eventually Chancellor Bonar Law intervened and the 'worst features of my persecution were … relaxed'. She was only finally discharged 'after the passage of the Franchise Bill'.[5]

Another area in which suffragettes cost the country significant sums was the window smashing campaign. On 29 June 1909, suffragette militancy had taken a new turn. Armed with small stones, thirteen women began systematically to break windows at the Privy Council, Treasury, and Home Office buildings. Unsurprisingly, the perpetrators were immediately arrested. These first broken panes were government property, but on 21 November 1911, whilst still targeting official buildings, the campaign was extended to shops, including department stores, and the offices of anti-suffrage papers, including *The Daily Mail* and *The Daily News*. What Emmeline Pankhurst called the 'argument of the broken pane' became amongst the most controversial of suffragette activities and alienated considerable support both inside and outside Parliament.

Sylvia Pankhurst graphically describes a 1 March 1912 event when,

> well-dressed women suddenly produced strong hammers from innocent-looking bags and parcels, and fell to smashing the shop windows. There is nothing like a hammer for smashing plate glass; stones, even flints, are apt to glance off harmlessly. The hammers did terrible execution … Damage amounting to thousands of pounds was effected in a few moments.[6]

Whilst this smashing orgy unfolded on London's main shopping streets, Emmeline Pankhurst calmly hailed a taxi and smashed a few windows of 10 Downing Street. The campaign continued during March, the military police were at times deployed to arrest perpetrators and, on one occasion in early March, 9,000 police were deployed in Trafalgar Square.

Not all women were convinced by this policy which Emmeline termed 'the most valuable argument in modern politics'.[7] Even some perpetrators were dubious, revisiting the shop whose windows they had broken to make a subsequent purchase – frequently a hat. When her niece Louisa was arrested, constitutionalist Millicent Fawcett wrote to Louisa's mother Elizabeth, 'I am in hopes she will take her punishment wisely, that the enforced solitude will help her to see more in focus than she always does.'[8] Louisa's case attracted significant press coverage, of the fourteen women arrested, she alone was named. Contrary to the antis' claim, Millicent denied being 'in the depths of despair' over the suffragettes' latest stunt, she simply continued to advocate using reason to promote the cause rather than 'attempting to grasp by violence what should be yielded' on the basis of 'justice'.[9]

Surprisingly, some leading London Department stores, despite their broken panes, continued to place advertisements for appropriate suffrage apparel for marches and processions in *Votes for Women*. (When women became war workers, advertisements simply reflected their new roles.) The then new and very modern Selfridges, whose proprietor was a known suffrage supporter, allegedly flew the WSPU flag atop the store when Emmeline was released from jail.[10] With so many WSPU members now drawn from the most privileged social classes for whom Selfridges catered, and with its rooftop restaurant a favourite WSPU meeting-place, he may have felt that their patronage outweighed the £60 (£6,300 today) cost of replacing two panes of glass.

If shop owners bore the cost of replacing their shattered windows (one placed a sign in his store 'Ladies, if we had the power to grant, you should have the Vote right away. Please don't smash these windows, they are not Insured'![11]), smashing government building windows and the deployment of additional police rendered the high profile campaign expensive to the government. Whilst less expensive, the concurrent, prolonged attacks on pillar boxes inconvenienced the public.

The first WSPU pillar box attack occurred on 26 November 1912. In a synchronised move, acid, ink, lampblack, and tar was poured into pillar boxes in the City of London, the West End, and several key provincial cities. In Newcastle alone, 2,000 letters were damaged.[12] In a society dependent on letters for most communications, this latest suffrage outrage sat ill with the public. In terms of the public purse, this campaign disrupted some government business and again used up police time with plainclothes policemen now guarding pillar boxes at key locations.

In June 1913, Margaret Mackworth, secretary of the Newport WSPU, daughter of suffrage-supporting former Liberal MP David Thomas, decided to nail her colours more prominently to the militant mask. Having collected the necessary paraphernalia at WSPU London headquarters, she returned to Newport to set about becoming an amateur incendiary-maker. Using a homemade bomb, she attempted to burn the contents of a pillar box on Risca Road. Ironically, 'burning letters was the one piece of militancy … of which I disapproved, I could not bear to think of people expecting letters and not getting them'.[13] She appeased her conscience by deciding that with the campaign well under way, people shouldn't post letters! She was arrested, tried, and found guilty. Due to her family background, the press had a field day. To his fury, she rejected her husband's (a Monmouthshire JP) offer to pay her fine, was imprisoned, went on hunger strike and was released after five days.

During the war Margaret, like anti-suffragist Violet Markham, worked for the Women's Department of the National Service Department, she took great pleasure in seeing recruiting posters for the WAACS placed on pillar boxes including the one she had targeted. In June 2015, a Blue Plaque was placed on the house adjacent to 'her' pillar box which, for the unveiling, was bedecked in the WSPU colours.[14]

No figures appear to exist regarding the overall cost to the Exchequer of these suffrage activities. Withheld taxes, smashed windows, scores of additional policemen guarding public buildings (and pillar boxes) and, when the arson campaign got under way, private property; police protection at public meetings and hustings, arrests, magistrates' and court time and the cost of imprisonment, forcible feeding and, after the Cat and Mouse Act, rearrests. All came with a heavy price tag. But during the war, some of these women who had collectively cost the government hundreds of thousands of pounds would be deeply involved with the Allied war effort, this time, at no or little cost to any government.

## Lena Ashwell (1872–1957) I am 'not a parenthesis'.

Few things in life are more certain than the requirement to pay taxes. To founder TRL member Lena Ashwell (a professional actress and theatre manager)'s fury, her 1913 income-tax demand was addressed not to her but to her husband. 'Dr H. J. Simpson, [*sic*], at her place of business the Kingsway Theatre, with the name "for wife" in brackets'. An 11 June 1913 article in *Derby Daily Telegraph* recounts her actions. At a meeting with Chancellor of the Exchequer Lloyd George, she argued that, 'anything that is a parenthesis … should not be on the list of those who support the work of this great nation [including] the Army, the Navy and the expected aeroplane'.[15] He seemingly agreed with her, claiming he felt it unjust that women played no part in 'framing laws they were deemed to obey'. Fourteen months after this meeting, Lena's 'great nation' was at war and she would make a significant contribution to the war effort. Reflecting post-war on her own and countless suffragists' pre-war and wartime endeavours, she concluded that, 'if there had not been the preparation of the suffrage movement, the women would have been able to do as little as in previous wars. … The women who had come out of comfortable homes and had suffered hardships were getting ready to fight a bigger battle to escape slavery.'[16]

Initially, the government seemed unable to harness the abilities of the countless women desperate to help the war effort. Lena, like hundreds of others, attended 'a great meeting … in the Albert Hall where leaders of the

Government addressed different groups of women. … It took a rather long time to say that the woman's place was the home.'[17]

By October 1914, having worked out how her talents could be used, Lena tried to arouse interest in her proposed entertainments for the troops and, with the backing of 'generals, bishops, distinguished musicians and actors, appealed to the War Office'.[18] Rebuffed, 'we were considered "useless"', she initially threw her energies into working for the Women's Emergency Corps.[19] Nevertheless, her original idea remained with her. Eventually, thanks to the intervention of Princess Helena Victoria and the Women's Auxiliary Committee of the YMCA, she was asked to send a concert party to Le Havre. Lena acknowledged that actors and Concert Parties were outside the comfort zone of this religious organisation relating how the YMCA were initially dubious 'as to what unknown terrors they were letting loose upon themselves. Some expected us to land in France in tights with peroxided hair'.[20] According to 19-year-old Elsie Griffin, the girls were locked into a caravan at night for their own protection.[21]

As the many stipulations included concerts not costing the government money, the first of countless fundraising events took place at the London Coliseum. Manager 'Oswald Stoll secured [for free] a company of artists whose usual rates would have amounted to over £5,000 (£525,000 today)'. The audience included Queens Alexandra and Mary, Princesses Mary and Helena Victoria, Prince Alexander of Teck and members of the diplomatic corps; 'tickets sold out well in advance, £1,450 (£152,500) was raised for each of the three parties'.[22] Keen to exploit the suffrage message, whenever Lena and other suffrage journalists wrote articles about the Concert Parties, they made the point that the 'women who had worked and struggled for women's political power were now placing their experience in organisation and routine-work on the altar of patriotism.'[23] Pre-war fundraising skills were exploited to the full; suffrage friends were roped in to provide or make goods for sales of work which, on occasion, were auctioned at the Savoy.

The first 'modern troubadours' arrived in France in early 1915; some were leading lights of the London stage, yet to the troops' amazement, they were prepared to brave knee-deep mud, candlelit huts, barns or tents, and for two hours, 'sing us the songs, the songs of our own land'.[24] To Lena's delight, doubts were almost immediately cast aside, it was obvious that artists had a very real part to play in terms of troop welfare and morale. Some men began to consider that other than a 'Blighty wound', a Lena Ashwell Concert Party was the best thing that could happen to them. Artistes performed in hospitals where, for a short while, they lightened the 'atmosphere impregnated with pain … and concentrated suffering' for patients, nurses and doctors – sometimes as many as 600; on one occasion in a Serious Cases Ward, a soldier died peacefully as the violinist played at his bedside.

Soon the originally cynical War Office regarded the 'Concert Parties' as making a crucial contribution to morale – but did not offer to defray expenses. A typical party consisted of four female and three male artistes, each would sing or play about fifty songs a day. An average of three parties went out every five weeks, visiting eleven bases and there were also three 'firing-line parties' that would perform within 800 yards of the German trenches. Some artistes gave their services gratis, others needed out of pocket expenses; all were billeted and provided with meals. A further expense occurred when the army decreed that artistes must wear YMCA uniforms paid for out of Concert Party funds. Whilst some people felt that a small entrance fee could be charged, Lena disagreed. To her, 'each note [sung] was a loving gift from home'.[25] Fundraising was, perforce, almost continuous; articles were written, publicity sought in newspapers, and meetings held in both public and private venues. At one event in Sheffield, nearly £2,000 (£180,000 today) was raised which was sufficient to pay for eighteen concerts; flag days were held with towns often raising money to send a party consisting of local artistes to 'their' boys. Contrary to their suffrage days, flag-sellers could stand on the pavement rather than in the gutter.

One modern troubadour, Ivor Novello, first performed 'Keep the Home Fires Burning' in the Harfleur valley. Lena remembered, 'When he sang it, the men seemed to drink it in at once and instantly sang the chorus, and as we drove away at the end of the concert, in the dark and the rain and the mud, from all parts of the camp one could hear the refrain.' Would this song, still synonymous with the First World War, ever have seen the light of day without the suffrage movement? Soon drama was added to the repertoire, Lena herself loved to perform Shakespeare – no one cared if this was in slightly unusual venues such as a horse hospital, or that heavy rain fell on patients wheeled out into the open air and on Lady Macbeth declaiming in their midst. Rain-drenched or not, Lena knew that 'the sight of our girls … [is] the very salt of life to these poor pain-wracked boys'.[26]

Troops serving in more distant theatres of war were not overlooked. Concert Parties headed for Malta (with its 20,000 hospital beds), Palestine and Egypt. In Cairo, audiences regularly exceeded 6,000 and Siegfried Sassoon based his poem 'Concert Party' on a concert given in the desert. Spellbound, 'we hear them, drink them, 'til the concerts done'. For Lena, the Mount of Olives was the most poignant venue. A concession was made to the weather, there was only one, not the usual two performances a day as singing in temperatures in excess of 120F was exhausting.

Lena Ashwell (by now OBE)'s most adventurous, and illegal, fundraising event occurred on 3, 4, 5 December 1917 at the Royal Albert Hall, scene of numerous suffrage meetings. Lotteries being 'illegal and yet by any other name might smell as sweet', it was dubbed a Petticoat Lane Tombola.[27] 'Admirable scarlet stations were found for advertisements for the event' namely pillar boxes.[28] It seemed that all society hostesses yearned to run a stall and a truly impressive array of £5,500 (£440,000 today) worth of prizes were donated including two acres of land on the Chiltern Hills (complete with the then equivalent of planning permission), a grand piano, a diamond necklace, a porcelain bathroom, but the prize which excited the most interest was 'a prize pedigree bull'.[29] However, this caused consternation amongst the office staff working round the clock to cope with the demand for tickets which cost 5s (£20). Where exactly does one tether a prize bull in Central London? ('There was no room for it in the Office'.) On the opening day, Mrs Asquith, the anti-suffrage wife of the former prime minister insisted on solemnly parading the bull round the Hall. So many tickets had been sold that they had to be mixed in a beer barrel lent by a brewery and a troop of boy scouts came and rolled the barrel to make sure the contents were thoroughly mixed. Admiral of the Fleet Lord Jellicoe drew the prizes but a frisson of anxiety went through the crowd when a policeman appeared. Would he declare the 'Tombola' a lottery and thus illegal? All was well, he had simply dropped in to see if he had a winning ticket.[30] A total of £34,000 (£2,706,400) was raised. During the four-year life of the Concert Parties at the Front, every means 'short of highway robbery' were used to keep the shows on the road and the troops entertained.[31]

Concerts continued post-war, both accompanying the Army of Occupation and entertaining soldiers impatiently awaiting demobilisation. Sadly, Emily Pickford (née Pearn) was one of three members who drowned in the Somme on the night of 9 February 1919. She lies with several other serving women in Abbeville Communal Cemetery in France. The soldiers considered these modern troubadours the 'fairy-godmother of us all'. Thanks to their founder and her network of suffrage supporters' unremitting fundraising efforts, 'Lena Ashwell's Concert Parties at Front', did not cost the government a penny.[32]

## Kathleen Burke (1887–1958) The '$1,000-a-day girl'.

The only child of a London and North-Western Railway Company official, 'who brought her up like a boy' and taught her stenography at the age of 10, several times great niece of Edmund Burke, Kathleen Burke's formative years were privileged.[33] Educated at Oxford and the Sorbonne, her facility with languages and (as yet undiscovered) public speaking gifts would be exploited to the full during the war. Staying with an uncle in America when war was declared, her return to England coincided with events unfolding in Scotland that would affect the rest of her life.

Pre-war, renowned Scottish surgeon Elsie Inglis had two driving passions: surgery and suffragism (Serbia eventually became the third); by 1900 Elsie was a passionate speaker and campaigner for female enfranchisement. In 1906, as a graduate of Edinburgh University, she unsuccessfully applied to vote for the two university MPs; in 1909, she became secretary of the Federation of the Scottish Suffrage Societies under the umbrella of the NUWSS. She considered militancy counter-productive and signed a public letter of protest against it. When war was declared, determined to link suffragism and surgery, Elsie contacted the Women's Hospital Corps only to find that they were fully staffed. She then offered her services to the Royal Army Medical Corps in Edinburgh, who instantly rebuffed her, 'Dear lady, Go home and sit still'. Sitting still was not amongst her many talents and so, backed by the Scottish Federation of Suffrage Societies and the wider NUWSS, she offered a fully equipped, all female hospital unit to Britain's allies. Known as the Scottish Women's Hospital Unit for Foreign Service (SWH), supported entirely by voluntary donations, units served in France, Serbia, Russia, Macedonia, Salonica and Corsica. Staffed by women from all suffrage societies, the SWH members proved that in war as well as in peace, women could do whatever needed to be done and, in their case, at no cost to the British Government.

Having arrived in England, Kathleen Burke, like many suffragists, proceeded to Belgium with the Women's Emergency Corps. She was appointed secretary to one of the first British commissions to Belgium, helping refugees flee to Britain before the German advance. Hinting at the shape of things to come, she managed to visit the battlefield at Melle and joined up with some soldiers 'cut off from their comrades in Mons' which provided her with excellent source material.[34] She left Ostend two days before Antwerp fell to the Germans in October 1914.

There is confusion in the records as to whether she returned to England or immediately proceeded to Serbia, where she was decorated with the Serbian Order of the Silver Eagle. By spring 1915, she was in England working as secretary in the SWH's London (Knightsbridge) office. Either because she herself was double-booked or thanks to her innate ability to spot talent in younger women and follow 'a hunch', in May 1915 Elsie Inglis set Kathleen on the path she would tread throughout the war.[35] Despite confessing to never having previously undertaken a public speaking engagement, she was dispatched to Oxford to replace Elsie and raise money for the SWH. She discovered a natural talent and was soon speaking the length and breadth of the land, generally hosted by suffrage societies, eloquently pleading the SWH cause and its never-ending need for funds to enable it to continue serving the French Army at the Abbé de Royaumont and with the Serb Army in the field. From June 1915, her name appears constantly in local British newspapers where she is billed as having just returned from 'the Front', 'talking charmingly', always reminding attendees that the NUWSS funded the hospitals. In August 1915, she was selected to receive the French Ambassador when he visited the SWH Knightsbridge office to inspect the 'magnificent travelling X-Ray motor car with entirely novel tent attachment' which, having cost £1,444 (£153,000 today), the London Committee was offering to France.[36] Kathleen had undoubtedly raised the lion's share.

In December 1915, Kathleen, who had now banked approximately £10,000 (over £1,000,000) for the SWH, shared a platform in Winchester with a rich American friend of her New York uncle. Spotting her gifts, this woman endeavoured to 'poach' her as a fundraiser for Serbia in America. Worried, Kathleen explained to the SWH treasurer, that this 'was a determined attempt to steal me from my present work'; she would not consider the scheme 'unless I saw a good profit coming to the Hospitals'.[37]

Having been received by the Serbian Ambassador in London who assured her that his countrymen 'will never forget all that the English and Scottish women had done for them' and with an agreement over fundraising reached, Kathleen set off on a three-month, 10,000 mile tour of Canada and America, her target was £10,000 (£940,000).[38] In a sexist comment, *The Daily Mirror* (19 January 1916) felt she had shown how 'good looks and business capacity can sometimes go together'.

Referring to her Irish Catholic roots, *The Tablet* noted in a lengthy article that on her first arrival in New York, Kathleen had initially been 'obstructed' by 'Pro-German Americans' whilst 'the Irish regarded her with much suspicion'. However, American audiences were soon as captivated as British ones; her quick wit and repartee delighted her listeners. Speaking on the New York Stock Exchange (an honour never hitherto accorded to a woman) she raised £2,000 (£188,000).[39]

At the end of this tour, the SWH were, according to 1 July 1916 *Jus Suffragii*, £12,000 (£1.1 million) the richer, enabling the SWH to make good on the promise that if sufficient funds were raised American donations would support an 'America Unit'. Andrew Carnegie donated £1,000 (£94,000) to this Unit which proved amongst the most successful of all SWH Units. American and Canadian newspaper dubbed her the '$1,000-a-day-girl' due to her spectacular fundraising success. Accounts of her speaking engagements show her deftly mixing women's rights to full citizenship with fundraising and she emphasised how the war had raised women's status. Headlines such as 'Miss Kathleen Burke Recently Returned From The Battle Front' drew crowds; pleading for audience sympathy, she frequently commented that she found pubic speaking more daunting than 'shells' of which, as she explained to her audience, she had experience.

With barely time to unpack her bags, Kathleen was off again. This time to Verdun, where she was slightly wounded. She was the first Englishwoman to enter what she called 'a white city of desolation'. Over 200,000 French and German soldiers lost their lives or were severely wounded and calculations indicate that during the offensive which lasted from 21 February until mid-July 1916, an average of 115 shells a minute fell on the citadel. Every normal sound had been replaced by the 'cruel sounds' of war. Having met Generals Nivelle, Pétain and Dubois and dined with General Joffre (they were as impressed by her as she with them), she felt that her time in the Sorbonne had helped her understand the French mentality whilst her stenography skills stood her in excellent stead for her ensuing hyperbolic book, *White Road to Verdun*. This proved another weapon in her fundraising arsenal. *Jus* delightedly tells readers that she reminded Pétain that the SWH was formed out of the suffrage movement before going on to add that it was no longer 'a question of politics but of serving humanity'.

Like all suffrage societies, the SWH London Committee had a well-oiled press cutting agency; they were no doubt gratified that her Verdun peregrinations attracted considerable press interest on both sides of the Atlantic. 29 August 1916 *Fort Scott Daily Tribune and Monitor*'s tone is typical, 'A mere slip of a girl ... Miss Burke stood calmly by the side of officers at Verdun while big shells were dropping about'. If, as *Jus* suggests, the visit was undertaken to provide additional material for her forthcoming speaking tours, such reports and photographs of her shaking hands with French generals proved invaluable. 22 August 1916 *Daily Mirror* waxed lyrical: Kathleen had been made an 'Officier de l'Instruction Publique des Beaux Arts'. Called by France a 'knight of tenderness and pity', she received France's 'Golden Palm' for her 'impressive eloquence' on behalf of wounded French and Serb soldiers.[40] By 9 September 1916, she was again crossing the Atlantic.

Unsurprisingly exhaustion soon set in. A millionaire friend offered to pay the SWH $1,000 if she would 'go down to his country place and stay quietly with his daughter' for two days. She delightedly told the Committee she had raised $1,000 by doing nothing, wishing 'some of the other millionaires would follow his example'.[41] Occasional hiccups were circumvented, when in San Francisco, some bureaucratic error prevented her from collecting her luggage, the outraged mayor appointed her 'special policeman', with a 5-pointed star inside her coat to prove it. She felt this might prove useful one day. Granted the freedom of several American cities, she was soon back in France, being mentioned in BEF Matron-in-Chief Maude McCarthy's 5 January diary entry which reported Kathleen had raised '£360,000 in America, in response to her many speeches' (nearly £23 million today). 'She ... has now been given permission by the A[djutant] G[eneral] to visit the English front, and I have been asked to accompany her ... with a conducting officer from GHQ.' In a carefully planned three-day tour, the women visited several forward Casualty Clearing Stations, Vimy Ridge – where 'one or two

Boche rifles and a divisional flag which we found in one of the dugouts' were acquired as souvenirs, providing useful props for Kathleen's final tour of the US undertaken in March 1918. Despite considerable bombardment, they visited Ypres, 'we were constantly stopped and asked whether we were in possession of steel helmets and gas helmets'.[42]

Leaving France on 8 January, according to *The Tablet* Kathleen 'braved the submarines and returned to America for a third time on a similar [equally successful] work of charity'. Accolades and additional Allied honours as well as money flooded in. Gazetted Honorary Colonel of the 138th US Field Artillery in recognition of her work for the American Red Cross, she was awarded the British CBE, became a knight of St Sava (Serbia) and a Chevalier of the *Légion d'honneur* (France). The young woman who told the SWH Committee that she was not sure if she had the skills to undertake that 1915 Oxford speaking engagement had surpassed all expectations and would have earned the highest praise that SWH founder Dr Elsie Inglis could bestow on any member of staff, 'Dear girl, I knew you could do it.'

## Evelina Haverfield (1867–1920) 'Always in Quest of a Cause'.

In March 1901, the Honourable Evelina Haverfield, boarded a troopship bound for South Africa to join her officer husband serving in the Boer War. A noted horsewoman, one of the first women in England to ride astride, she soon became concerned about army horses abandoned on the veldt. The initiative, total commitment, organisational and administrative skills she demonstrated whilst establishing a horse retirement 'home' proved invaluable during her suffrage and subsequently war service years in England and Serbia. Her knowledge of military organisation, acquired when her husband became a District Commissioner, would also pay dividends. Shocked by the conditions facing civilians as well as horses, she returned from South Africa mentally and physically tough, 'a seasoned veteran confident in her abilities to do something personally to change and improve situations'.[43]

Evelina joined a Dorset branch of the NUWSS in the 1890s. If her path had not already crossed that of NUWSS president Millicent Fawcett, it did so in South Africa. Evelina's doctor sister Ella was a member of the commission which Millicent headed following Emily Hobhouse's allegations regarding concentration camp conditions. By 1908, Evelina had also joined the WSPU becoming a generous benefactor as well as a deeply committed member and honorary secretary of the Sherborne WSPU.[44] She marched in numerous suffragette processions, undertook speaking engagements and was involved in the June 1913 pageant – her equine knowledge useful when dealing with carthorses!

In June 1909 Evelina was arrested for being one of the deputation of women who, claiming it was their constitutional right to petition the prime minister, sought entry to the House of Commons. Brought to trial and defended by suffrage-supporting Lord Robert Cecil, she, along with Emmeline Pankhurst, was found guilty and fined – her fine was paid without her consent. Her next brush with the authorities occurred on Black Friday 1910 when, acting as 'security guard', she rode behind the deputation Emmeline led to Parliament. As the ugly situation became uglier, 'Cutting through the crowds, she swung her crop in the faces of the officers, knocking many down; she had created a break in the police line'.[45] Charged with assault, she agreed she had struck a policeman in the mouth and threatened 'next time to bring a revolver'.[46] The following year, she put her ability to force horses to sit down by hitting them near the joint of their hind legs to good use when police horses were used during the window smashing campaign. A two-week prison sentence followed; this bothered her not at all although it is possible that her aristocratic antecedents prompted her early release. A founder member of the TRL, she left the WSPU in 1914, joined Sylvia Pankhurst's ELF and became its honorary treasurer.

On the declaration of war, Evelina, whom the public saw as 'that awful suffragette', directed her energies towards the 'German threat'.[47] An excellent markswoman, she longed to establish a Women's Rifle Corps but, when this proved a non-starter, looking 'every inch the soldier', she joined the Women's Emergency Corps, became Honorary Colonel of the Women's Volunteer Reserve and then plunged into the Women's Reserve Ambulance. Initially, her name appears in multiple military-style women's corps. Uniformed war work on the Home Front now replaced her ardent suffragism. In December 1914, 'always in quest of a cause', she threw in her lot with the SWH; knowing that every penny raised was precious, she volunteered for Serbia at her own expense.[48] As happened with SWH founder Elsie Inglis, Serbia would henceforth define Evelina's life.

Despite her numerous 'honorary' roles, Evelina had never held a professional post, nor did she have any knowledge of hospitals but Elsie seemingly felt that her proven ability to cope with hardship, her initiative, energy and undoubted courage would compensate for any shortcomings – which included a tendency to both experiencing and provoking violent antipathy as well as intense loyalty. She was appointed Hospital Administrator. Both sides of her charismatic character were soon fully displayed in this role and her subsequent one as head of the Transport Section.

In Serbia, against the background of the bitter fighting of 1915, Evelina completed the highly complex task of establishing sites, staff accommodation, transport and supplies for four of the hospitals which the SWH were providing for Serb wounded. Many considered Evelina, with her ability to work for twenty-two hours a day and sleep on the roadside if needs be, both capable and indefatigable. SWH members commented that Evelina and Elsie had the energy of '20 horses apiece'. When Bulgaria invaded Serbia in late 1915, they were amongst the last women to evacuate; all the returning SWH received much press adulation – a change for suffragette Evelina who was more used to journalistic opprobrium.

Like so many SWH volunteers, Evelina embarked on multiple fundraising missions before returning to Serbia in July 1916 as head of the Transport Section – a surprising role for a woman who does not appear to have either owned or even driven a car. The Section comprised eight ambulances, two kitchen cars, one repair car, four lorries, three touring cars, twenty-two drivers, two cooks and fifty tons of donated equipment. Hardships, which Evelina took in her stride, immediately became part of everyday life. She told the London Committee, 'We slept in the lorries and ambulances ... and reached our destination in pouring rain and blowing half a gale'.[49] Pushing and heaving lorries and ambulances on roads which had disappeared under a quagmire of mud, always with a care for the wounded who were now pouring in, was part of life. Frequently bombed from the air and shelled from the ground, the drivers' immense courage and outward calmness was inspirational. Elsie noted how Evelina's Column, constantly within range of the guns, was 'out at all hours, never too tired to turn out, always gentle and careful and always cheerful'.[50] Inevitably, many of the women who in one Column member's opinion were 'too young or too delicate for the job', reached breaking point, possibly including Evelina who drove herself even harder than she drove her staff.[51] Elsie Bowerman, whose family knew Evelina well, concluded that she was under unbearable strain. It is tempting to diagnose shell-shock as she appeared at times unstable and prone to incontrollable bursts of anger.

To add to the Column's stresses, Evelina and one of the doctors, Lilian Chesney, were on collision course. Lilian was known to be as prone to strong likes and dislikes as Evelina and the atmosphere between these two strong-minded women became poisonous. Eventually deciding that she could less easily sacrifice a doctor and with Transport Column members resigning, Elsie, herself a hard taskmaster, accepted that the Column was being driven too hard. She tactfully sent Evelina home whilst acknowledging her superb achievements, 'The success of the transport was due to 2 things: the pluck and staying power of the girls and [Evelina's] splendid powers of initiative and indomitable spirit. Very few other women could have put it through.'[52]

Back in England in early April 1917, Evelina embarked on successful fundraising tours; she threw herself into these with the same commitment she had shown to every cause she had ever espoused. The SWH London Committee expressed themselves in awe of her achievements and dedication. Her thoughts soon returned to Serbia and suffering Serb soldiers, leading to further fundraising, this time for 'Sergeant-Major Flora Sandes and Evelina Haverfield's Fund for Promoting Comforts for Serb Soldiers and Prisoners'; fellow suffragette Nina Boyle was also on the Committee. Nina and Evelina used their suffrage connections as well as their speaking skills and frontline experiences to boost the Fund's coffers.

As with several British women who had served in Serbia, the country and its overwhelming sufferings still exerted a pull over Evelina. In December 1918, she became Commissioner of the Serbian Red Cross Society. Speaking fluent if ungrammatical Serbian, she returned to Serbia to set up an orphanage for the thousands of orphaned and war-displaced children. Dr Isobel Hutton, chief of the 'America' SWH Unit met her in 1919. Awed by Evelina's dedication, she commented that nothing was too much for her, 'she always chose for herself the hardest and most difficult way', adding, 'We all fell under the spell of her charm and radiant smile.'[53] Serb orphans were Evelina's last cause. She died of pneumonia in 1920. Respecting her final request, she was buried in Bajina Bashta, 'in a field where horses can walk over me'.[54]

Organised by Serbs, Croats and Slovenes, the memorial service for Evelina Haverfield, holder of the Order of St Sava and (posthumously) the

Order of the White Eagle (with Swords) took place in London's Southwark Cathedral. Attended by members of the many organisations whose lives she had deeply touched, her legacy is ongoing. Her orphanage is now part of a large health complex and a wall plaque pays tribute to the memory of 'a noble Englishwoman who gave her life … for the sake of our people'. She is one of the six women who feature on the beautiful stamps Serbia issued in 2015 to commemorate 'British Heroines of the First World War'. Funded by an army of largely suffrage fundraisers, these women's service and their commitment to Britain's ally, 'Gallant Little Serbia', cost neither the British nor Serb governments a penny.

## Mary Borden (1886–1968) 'with black blood upon her face'.

On 3 March 1917, *Brooklyn Life* featured a long article entitled 'An American Prototype of the Immortal Florence Nightingale'. With graphic descriptions of frontline nursing, this was an appeal for funds for the 'most important Field Hospital with the French Army, Mary Borden-Turner's 4,000 bed Hôpital de l'Evacuation'. The article praised her as 'the finest example of American womanhood', but made no mention of her involvement with English suffragism.

Daughter of a Chicago millionaire father and Christian fundamentalist mother, Mary (known as May), had attended Vassar College which accepted only high achieving students and produced strong, independent women. She lived up to Vassar's expectations and excelled not only in her academic studies but also at inter-collegiate debates where she tested and aired many of her firmly held beliefs. By the time she graduated in 1907 she had inherited a significant fortune from her father. Whilst her mother longed for her daughter to be a missionary, May wanted to become a writer. Hoping this would push her in the right direction, Mrs Borden arranged a world tour which included visiting some of the many overseas missions founded by the Bordens.

In India, May met and subsequently married an Anglo–Indian missionary, Douglas Turner. After five years in India, the now unhappily married couple and their two daughters settled in London in early 1913. In May 1913, private member Willoughby Dickinson introduced a Women's Franchise Bill to the House of Commons, defeated on a second reading by forty-seven votes. Opposing it Asquith stated that 'woman is not the female of the human species, but a distinct and inferior species'.[55] In response, suffragette militancy increased: shop windows, mansions, pillar boxes, tennis courts and golf courses were targeted. "'Dummy" bombs left on the underground and in public buildings, real bombs manufactured and used in arson attacks', and interrupted church services were almost routine; the value of damage by arson in 1913 alone was around £510,150 (£53 million today).[56] With her educational background and feminist instincts (demonstrated in her 1912 novel *The Mistress of the Kingdom*), it is no surprise to find May involved with English suffragism.

Despite being uncertain about militancy, in autumn 1913, May joined hundreds of women from across the country who foregathered outside Parliament. She was selected to fling a stone through the windows of the Treasury Buildings. Although to her dismay, two stones fell wide of the target, the third, with the police closing in upon her, satisfyingly found its target. Unsurprisingly, she was arrested. She spent five nights in a prison cell before her husband paid her 25s fine and she was released, which she ruefully acknowledged saved her from hunger-striking.

When war was declared, Douglas volunteered as interpreter with the Indian troops. Heavily pregnant, May gave her name to the London Committee of the French Red Cross, declaring her willingness to become a volunteer nurse, despite having no professional nursing skills and only a basic knowledge of French. Her can-do attitude was such that she felt that neither of these deficits, nor her pregnancy, created insurmountable barriers.

In January 1915, recently delivered of her third daughter, May went to Dunkirk to a grim hospital in a former casino where typhus was rampant and French poilus were being nursed in horrific conditions resembling those of the Crimea War. May was horrified, particularly at the lack of night staff, and when a drunken orderly was placed in sole charge of two wards, she snapped. Breaking all French hospitals rules about women and night nursing, she organised a rota of night staff amongst the English volunteers.[57] Having fallen foul of the French nursing authorities she hatched a plan to develop her own Unit embedded with the French Army; she, May, would be directrice.

May estimated that it would cost about £4,000 (£424,000 today) to set the hospital up with monthly running costs of £200 (£21,200). She would pay to establish this, the French would merely assist with the day-to-day running costs. To help raise money, she relinquished the lease on her London house, and moved herself, her American investments, her three daughters and a nanny to Paris. Drawing on her literary abilities and on her experiences in Dunkirk, May wrote, and continued to write, graphic articles and pleas for funds which were placed in American newspapers. In July 1915, Hôpital Chirurgical Mobile No. 1, with twelve long wooden portable huts with reinforced windows to take the strain of heavy firing, was up and running. Like all mobile (field) hospitals, it could be packed up and transported with only a few hours' notice.

Initially established on the Dunkirk/Ypres road, May recruited all the nursing staff, some hailed from Australia, others from her native America; those who did not meet her exacting standards were asked to leave; others remained for the duration. Soon wounded officers and men pleaded to be sent there, the hospital's low mortality rate of five per cent was becoming renowned. Winter of 1915 was grim for patients, staff and directrice. With the weather lashing the flimsy huts, May slept beneath a 'mackintosh sheet with an umbrella over her head'.[58] Guns and shellfire, the constant musical accompaniment.

As the French field of military operations moved further south, May longed to accompany them; eventually General Joffre, whom she had been bombarding with passionate if ungrammatical letters, held up the white flag of surrender. In October 1915, she was given permission to establish a 2,000 bed Hôpital de l'Evacuation at Bray-sur-Somme. It would soon be directly in the war zone. By the time the hospital was fully operational, May described it in a (fundraising) letter as, 'A city of huts, and the guns beyond the hill sound like the waves of the sea, pounding – pounding – and the sky is a whirr with aeroplanes and sometimes we are bombarded and all the time troops and more troops stream past'.[59] All too soon these troops would stream back as casualties, disfigured, maimed and with their wits as shattered as their bodies. Determined that her patients would have the best care that she and her thirteen nurses could give, she often fell foul of the French military authorities. Outraged that a wounded man's uniform was considered more important to preserve than his life, she overruled the order that uniforms should be preserved for future use. At her hospital, these would be cut through with knives or scissors to try to avoid inflicting additional pain on the already pain-crazed casualties.

Feminist May considered her hospital as the second battlefield where women fight to save the lives that the first (male) battlefield had tried to destroy. A battle that she described as a counter-wave of life to create the ebb against the flow. A battle that she would often win – her mortality rate was half the thirty per cent expected of French frontline facilities in this area. She was far from alone in seeing and writing about the irony of women saving men's lives so that they could simply fight and be wounded again.

May's wartime private life was as tumultuous and as gender-reversed as her public one. In 1916, she was introduced to Captain Edward Louis Spears, attached to the Staff Office and thus away from the Front Line. He was something rare on the Somme Front – a whole man with all his limbs, eyes, ears and even a nose intact. His first glimpse of her was of a 'small woman in a mud-splattered and blood-stained apron'.[60] Before long, May's burdens of nursing, running a hospital for which she was constantly fundraising, writing short stories and poems (arguably she is amongst the finest war poets of either gender), were supplemented by an illicit love affair. Bemused by Louis's passion, in one of her many magnificent sonnets to him she wondered, how 'can a man adore / A woman with black blood upon her face,' her hands 'dripping with the slimy dead'.[61] Whilst her love poetry was private, she, like so many other poets was finding an outlet for her torment in war poetry which started appearing in *English Review* in summer 1917.[62] With her hospital so close to the Front Line, she saw the first tanks lumbering down the road at Flers in September 1916, immortalising in 'The Hill' these 'obscene crabs, armoured toads, … crushing under their bellies whatever stood in their way'.

May's courage and devotion to her wounded poilus had not gone unnoticed. In March 1917, she was cited in French Army Orders for her courage and steadfastness. One of very few American women to receive the Croix de Guerre, to which a 'palme' was added by General Pétain for her hospital work, this was soon followed with, to her bemusement, the *Légion d'honneur*.

In June 1917, the hospital was transferred to Roesbrugge, twenty miles from Passchendaele. Overwhelmed by the never-ending stream of hideously wounded men, in her poetry, May and her patients' sufferings merge into an orgy of mental and physical anguish,

Their wounds gape at me – Their stumps menace me; Their bandaged faces grimace at me; Their death rattle curses me … I am stained, I am soiled, I am streaked with their blood, I am soaked with the odour of the oozing of their wounds – I am saturated with the poison of their poor festering wounds, I am poisoned, I'm infected – I am heavy with the weight of my helpless wounded men.[63]

In the appalling conditions of the Third Battle of Ypres (Passchendaele), May's writings indicate a woman under almost unbearable strain, 'obsessed by the obscenity of war'. However, her attempts to publish a mainly prose, war-inspired collection proved futile: censors considered some pieces damaging to morale and requested their removal. She refused and *The Forbidden Zone* only appeared in 1929.

Ill-health, almost certainly resulting from years of constant strain, caused not only by the conditions in which she was nursing but by running and constantly fundraising for the hospital, not to mention an ever more complicated affair with Louis which ended in her divorce, led May to relinquish hospital work in late 1917. Having married Louis in March 1918, in recognition of her service to the French Army, she joined General Pétain for the Strasbourg Victory Parade on 25 November and dined with George V at the British Embassy in Paris. Keeping open house in her Parisian home during the Peace Conference, she heard delegates who attended her soirées thrashing out finer points of the various Peace Treaties. One remark made significant impact upon her, the Polish prime minister's wife 'clutched my hand and gasped, "My dear child – what a different world."'[64]

The world dawning in June 1919 was indeed a very 'different' one to the one envisaged by slightly reluctant militant suffragette, May Borden-Turner who, in the autumn of 1913, had lobbed a stone through the Treasury buildings and spent five nights in police custody. Like so many women, May had called upon previously unimaginable fundraising skills, determination, fortitude, and dedication to achieve the goal she had set herself at Dunkirk in early 1915. Other dreams remained less fulfilled, women's enfranchisement had been but partially realised, whilst the gender equality in which she so intensely believed was still little more than a chimera.

# Conclusion: Dreams (Un)fulfilled

The 1918 Representation of the People Act passage through Parliament was far from smooth. Its parliamentary advocates knew that some suffragists would find the age qualification unacceptable and from October 1916 until the January 1917 Speaker's Conference, attempts were made to sweeten the pill. In December 1916, Millicent Fawcett had acknowledged that some compromise over women's voting age was necessary, reluctantly concurring with leading suffragist MP W. H. Dickinson that acceptance would 'avoid the risk of the Government having an excuse for saying that, as it is impossible to satisfy the advocates of W[omen's] S[uffrage], they refrain from dealing with W.S. at all'.[1] Pragmatic as ever, Millicent subsequently wrote to Prime Minister Lloyd George explaining that, 'We should greatly prefer an imperfect scheme that can pass, to the most perfect scheme in the world that could not pass.'[2]

With limited Suffrage Victory within grasp, many agreed with her. Tax Resister Evelyn Sharp believed, 'the happiest moment of my life was ... on the evening when the Reform Bill received the Royal Assent'; this was 'the bloodless triumph of a fight for human freedom'.[3] Despite war still raging, German suffragists penned their congratulations believing that English women's partial enfranchisement 'promises us, too, ultimate victory'.[4] In the manner so singularly her own, Emmeline Pankhurst claimed the victory solely for the WSPU. She omitted to mention the multiple societies involved in the long and painful struggle and simply asserted (for decades this became the received wisdom) that, 'the WSPU by its pre-war crusade for the Vote, followed by its patriotic stand and national service during the War, has won the greatest political victory on record'.[5]

Others were less euphoric. An outraged Sylvia Pankhurst expressed concerns for the approximately 6 million still disenfranchised women. She and WFL members including Charlotte Despard held 'aloof from rejoicings; they stride with a hollow and unreal sound upon our consciousness'.[6] With the partial franchise having been extended 'in a grudging spirit', Sylvia aspired to Parliament being replaced by 'Councils of Workers'. NUWSS member Eleanor Rathbone (elected to Parliament in 1929) considered the recommendations were far from 'satisfactory as such a Franchise would be of no use to the [female] factory worker'.[7] Fears soon proved well-founded. In its 'Annual Report 1919', the National Union of Societies for Equal Citizenship (NUSEC), formerly the NUWSS, presciently anticipated that far from the parliamentary franchise having protected women's rights, 'there is real and imminent danger of many of those careers, professions and trades which have been open to women being once again closed to them'. By the 1920s, NUSEC's Parliamentary Secretary Eva Hubback was convinced that the exclusion of working–class women had 'shut [them] out' from any 'advantages' of the franchise.[8]

It was becoming increasingly obvious that the hopes for equality pinned on even partial female enfranchisement were ill-founded. It was not only disenfranchised factory or working-class women who were deriving no benefit from women's voting rights; so profound was the post-war misogynistic backlash that professional women were vulnerable, even medical schools re-imposed restrictions on numbers of women entrants.[9] The NUSEC's 1921 Annual Report admitted that 'women's questions are for the moment in the trough of the wave' and feared that 'real equality' was not even on the distant horizon. In 1926, the NUSEC had little good news to share in its annual report, 'the lack of parliamentary progress regarding Equal Franchise has been a very depressing factor'.

Then, almost to the NUSEC's surprise, on 27 May 1927 in the Albert Hall, scene of so many suffrage meetings, Prime Minister Stanley Baldwin announced that he intended to honour his 1924 election pledge of Equal Franchise. A majority vote in favour of the measure was not a foregone conclusion. Women's representatives, with their long experience of promises broken and bills shelved, knew there was strong Cabinet opposition. Some politicians (and newspapers) were scathing about what they termed 'the flapper vote'. With an eye to party politics, Winston Churchill 'wished the proposal had been postponed by the Cabinet' but consoled himself that women were as likely as men to vote Conservative.[10] To the veteran suffrage campaigners, it was irrelevant which party younger women might choose to support, only their right to do so mattered. Lady Rhondda, imprisoned in

1913 for planting an incendiary in a pillar box, and, having recently inherited her father's peerage, had been fighting F. E. Smith (Alice Wheeldon's persecutor), now Lord Birkenhead, for the right to take up her hereditary seat in the House of Lords, spearheaded the campaign for 'Equal Political Rights' and the removal of the female age and property bar.

Determined to 'help Mr Baldwin to keep his pledge', the old suffrage mechanisms were once again deployed.[11] A 'Great Demonstration' was organised in Trafalgar Square on 16 July 1927. The stalwarts of decades of fierce campaigns lent their support, including octogenarians Charlotte Despard and Millicent Fawcett.[12] Charlotte, 'in the late evening of my life', rejoiced at once again addressing crowds from Nelson's Column. Youth was represented by 21-year-old Ida whose father, the Liberal MP and former Home Secretary Sir Herbert Samuel, had so totally dropped his opposition to female enfranchisement that in October 1918 he moved the motion for women to be eligible to stand as MPs. Forty women's organisations – including Trades Union and suffrage – turned out in force. Veteran campaigners wore their prison medals, none more proudly than those bearing the 'Hunger-Strike' clasp.

On 11 May 1928, the feminist journal *Time and Tide* triumphantly announced, 'AN EQUAL FRANCHISE BILL [has passed] its third reading in the House of Commons without division and even without comment'. Two weeks later its editor Lady Rhondda reported that, winding up the debate in the Upper Chamber, Lord Birkenhead had reluctantly advised their lordships to 'go into the Lobby in favour of this Bill, if without enthusiasm, yet in a spirit of resolute resignation'.

Watched by the 19-year-old Millicent Garrett (Fawcett), the opening salvo in the battle for women's enfranchisement had been fired in 1866. Now, sixty-two years later, the long and acrimonious struggle was finally over. Suffragists had fought their campaign during both peace and war. Their ranks had been spilt and friendships destroyed or cemented by the world's most bitter conflict, as, according to their consciences, women had supported or hindered the war effort. Post-war, some had buried the hatchet determined to continue the franchise struggle to the end; for others, the perceived betrayals including the acceptance of the 1918 limited franchise, went too deep. Yet on one point they all agreed: the parliamentary franchise would improve women's and children's lives. No longer demeaned as an 'inferior species' but acknowledged as equal citizens, women would now, just as they had always done and never more visibly than during the war, contribute to and enrich every aspect of national life including the political.

Yet in the century after the 1918 and 1928 Acts, the 'gender gap' still exists. Only in 1970 was Sylvia Pankhurst and countless other suffragists' dream of 'Equal Pay' enshrined in Law – but there is still a significant difference in men's and women's lifetime earnings and there are only seven female directors of FTSE 100 Companies. Thanks to ongoing campaigning by the Fawcett Society, by April 2018 UK employers with over 250 employees will be required by law to report their gender pay gaps. Women in the highest ranks in the Armed Services are still thin on the ground. A century after the formation of the WAAC, out of the eighteen regular army brigades, there appear to be no female commanders; there is one female air vice-marshal, the navy has one female commander (Faslane Naval Base).[13] In 2017, only twenty-nine per cent of police officers and twenty-four per cent of High Court judges were female. In 2008, the British press reported what it considered a 'worrying rise of women in medicine'; in September 2016, 'Senior medical leaders criticised the Government's "unacceptable" admission that the new junior doctors contract will have a disproportionate [negative] impact on women'.[14] Eleven of the UK's Anglican Community's seventy bishops are female, all but two in 'suffragan' (junior) positions. In the 2017 General Election the greatest number of female MPs ever was elected – but they still only account for thirty-one per cent of parliamentarians and out of twenty-three Cabinet Ministers, just six (twenty-six per cent) including the prime minister are women. Whilst the centenaries of the 1918 Representation of the People and the 1928 Equal Franchise Acts are rightly celebrated, 'the fight for full equality remains as vital as ever'.[15]

# Endnotes

## Chapter One: 'Getting ready to fight a bigger battle'

1. See *inter alia* Millicent Garrett Fawcett *The Women's Victory and After 1911–1918* p. 151
2. Ray Strachey *The Cause* p. 365
3. Fawcett p. 151; also in Strachey p. 366
4. John Sutherland *Mrs Humphrey Ward Eminent Victorian Pre-eminent Edwardian* p. 364
5. Fawcett p. 150
6. Fawcett p. 150; Sutherland p. 364
7. Vera Brittain *Testament of Youth* Virago, 1985 p. 404–5
8. Extract from Queen Victoria's letter to Prince Albert's biographer, in ed Joyce Marlowe *Suffragettes* p. 17
9. Ed Betty Balfour *Letters of Lady Constance Lytton* p. 125
10. Edmund Turner in *The American Political Science Review*, Vol. 7, No. 4 (Nov., 1913), pp. 588-609 Published by: American Political Science Association Stable URL: http://www.jstor.org/stable/1944309 p. 588
11. Quoted in Turner p. 589
12. Andrew Rosen *Rise Up, Women!* p. 6
13. Rosen p. 7
14. William Gladstone *Letter on Female Suffrage to Samuel Smith, MP*, 1892
15. Kate Frye *Diary* February 1907
16. See Harold Smith *The British Women's Suffrage Campaign 1866–1928* p. 11
17. Strachey p. 318
18. Elizabeth Crawford *The Women's Suffrage Movement: A Reference Guide* 2001 p. 216
19. http://metro.co.uk/2016/06/14/emmeline-pankhurst-suffragette-who-helped-give-women-the-vote-5942418/#ixzz4lgzeHVok
20. See Crawford p. 1036
21. Stephen Bates Asquith p. 135

22. Rosen p. 114; 211-212

23. Martin Pugh *Women's Suffrage in Britain, 1867–1928* p. 25

24. Rosen p. 12 (1884-1897 was 'the nadir of the women's suffrage movement in Britain')

25. Brian Harrison *Separate Spheres* p. 83

26. Martine Faraut (2003) Women resisting the vote: a case of anti feminism?, *Women's History Review*, 12:4, 605-621 p. 605

27. Faraut p. 605

28. Lisa Tickner *The Spectacle of Women: Imagery of the Suffrage Campaign 1907–1914* p. 59

29. Strachey p. 307

30. https://www.nytimes.com/interactive/2017/01/22/us/politics/womens-march-trump-crowd-estimates.html https://www.theguardian.com/us-news/2017/jan/21/donald-trump-first-24-hours-global-protests-dark-speech-healthcare

31. Strachey p. 308

32. Strachey p. 306

33. Ed. Elizabeth Crawford *Campaigning for the Vote Kate Frye's Suffrage Diary* 2013 p. 29

34. The most comprehensive list of suffrage colours can be found in Lisa Tickner *The Spectacle of Women: Imagery of the Suffrage Campaign 1907–1914*

35. Diane Atkinson *The Suffragettes in Pictures* p. 120

36. Margaret Mackworth *This Was My World* p. 118

37. Rhondda p. 118

38. Rhondda p. 119

39. Crawford p. 22

40. Beatified 1909, canonised 1920

41. http://www.historicalpageants.ac.uk/featured-pageants/sherborne-pageant-1905/

42. Cicely Hamilton *A Pageant of Great Women* 1910 p. 16

43. *Votes for Women* 'An Army with Banners' 15 July 1910

44. See Tickner p. 55-56 and ff.

45. One of Sir John French's widowed sisters. Fawcett p. 58

46. Crawford p. 549

47. See Crawford p. 550

48. Dora Sigerson Shorter, 'The Vagrant's Heart' first published in *The Troubadour and Other Poems*

49. Between 1906 and 1914 c. 1,085 suffragettes were imprisoned see Paula Bartley *Votes for Women* 2011 edition p. 118

50. Eliza Vaughan Essex Records Office

51. Crawford p. 553

52. https://sheroesofhistory.wordpress.com/2015/09/03/katherine-harley/

53. https://sheroesofhistory.wordpress.com/2015/09/03/katherine-harley/

54. *Anti-Suffrage Review* quoted by Tickner p. 235

55. Diarist Elsie Bowerman when serving with the SWH in Russia made several such annotations

56. See Fawcettt p. 59

57. Rosen p. 252

58. Atkinson p. 173

59. See Tickner pp. 232 ff

60. Arthur Marwick *Women at War* p. 55

61. See Deborah Thom *Nice Girls and Rude Girl Women Workers in World War One* 1998 p. 86

62. R. Mitchell 'A monstrous regiment of women: adding nineteenth century women to the new *DNB' Oxford DNB Newsletter* 1 3-4

**Chapter Two: Hunger for Change**

1. 16 October 1905 *Manchester Guardian*

2. Working-class women nearly always ended up in the Second Division, initially, more privileged women were more likely to be sent to the First Division.

3. See William Harman 'The Forcible Feeding Of Suffrage Prisoners' *The Lancet* Volume 180, No. 4644, p. 671–672, 31 August 1912

4. https://womenshistorynetwork.org/excluded-from-the-record-women-refugees-and-relief-1914-1929 June 2017

5. Katherine Storr *Excluded from the Record Women Refugees and Relief 1914-1929* p. 54. My thanks to Nathalie Trouveroy, wife of HE Guy Trouveroy, Belgian Ambassador to the UK 2014-2017, for additional information about Lelaing, something of a known dandy.

6. See *Alison Woodeson*, (1993) 'The first women police: a force for equality or infringement?', Women's History Review, 2:2, pp. 217–32. p. 222

7. Mary Allen *The Pioneer Policewoman (PP)* p. 10

8. P. Levine '"Walking the streets in a way no decent woman should": Women police in World War I', *Journal of Modern History*, 66 (1994), 34–78 p. 57

9. Woodeson p. 222

10. Joan Lock *The British Policewoman her Story* p. 21

11. Mary Allen *Lady in Blue (LIB)* pp.12–13

12. Allen *LIB*. pp 21-22

13. Quoted in Nina Boyd *From Suffragette to Fascist: The Many Lives of Mary Sophia Allen* p. 38

14. See Boyd p. 40

15. Allen *LIB*. p. 18

16. Boyd p. 43

17. Allen *PP* p. 13

18. Allen *PP* p. 22

19. Allen *PP* p. 26

20. Allen *PP* p. 26

21. Allen *PP* p. 29-30

22. Allen *PP* p. 25

23. See Boyd. p. 63

24. John Carrier 'The Control of women by women: The Women Police, *The Society for the Study of Labour History* 26 (1973) p. 17

25. *The Vote* 1 January 1915

26. Her personal account of these events is held in the IWM EMP 41/1 Women's Collection

27. Allen *PP* p. 41

28. Allen *PP* p. 60

29. Allen *PP* p. 104

30. Gabrielle West's diaries are held at the IWM

31. http://212.62.21.14/Article/Women-in-the-Police/1400015656544/1400015656544

32. Carrier p. 18

33. Allen *LIB* p. 50

34. *The Times* 3 November 1922

35. Elizabeth Crawford *The Women's Suffrage Movement: A Reference Guide* p. 75

36. See http://spartacus-educational.com/boyleN.htm

37. https://en.wikipedia.org/wiki/Cressida_Dick

38. Nicholas Hiley, 'Internal Security in Wartime: The Rise and Fall of PMS2, 1915 – 1917', *Intelligence and National Security*, 1986, vol. 1, issue 3. Hiley argues

that when Alice was incarcerated, mounting left-wing agitation over the case led to the closure of PMS2' pp. 408-410

39. http://www.heanorhistory.org.uk/suffragettes.html

40. Quoted in Sylvia Rowbotham *Friends of Alice Wheeldon* p. 5

41. See http://www.derbyshirelife.co.uk/out-about/places/the-village-of-breadsall-derbyshire-1-1630424

42. See David Doughan, 'Wheeldon, Alice Ann (1866–1919)', *Oxford Dictionary of National Biography*, Oxford University Press, 2004; online edn, Jan 2008 [http://www.oxforddnb.com/view/article/67034,] hereafter *ODNB*

43. Rowbotham p. 34, see also Karyn Burnham *The Courage of Cowards*

44. Rowbotham p. 40

45. Rowbotham. p. 43

46. See *inter alia* Rowbotham p. 47

47. See Rowbotham p. 52

48. *John Jackson*, 'Losing the Plot: Lloyd George, F.E. Smith and the trial of Alice Wheeldon', *History Today*, May 2007, p. 45; see also Nicola Rippon, *The Plot to Kill Lloyd George: The Story of Alice Wheeldon and the Peartree Conspiracy*

49. Basil Thomson *The Story of Scotland Yard* p. 238

50. Quoted in John Jackson 'Alice Wheeldon and the Attorney-General; 18 April 2007 in www.opendemocracy.net/globalization-institutions_government/wheeldon_attorney_4540.jsp

51. Alice Wheeldon ODNB

52. Rowbotham p. 80

53. Adam Hochschild, *To End All Wars: How the First World War Divided Britain* p. 313.

54. Alice Wheeldon ODNB http://theworldismycountry.info/posters/poster-3-alice-wheeldon-was-a-prophet

55. www.opendemocracy.net/globalization-institutions_government/wheeldon_attorney_4540.jsp

56. Gina Sigillito *Daughters of Maeve: 50 Irish Women Who Changed the World* p. 87

57. David Mitchell *Women on the Warpath* p. 350

58. For an outline of the links between Gore-Booth and Christabel Pankhurst see Crawford op. cit. p. 249 and 487

59. Mitchell p. 350

60. *ODNB* provides a fascinating account of Markiewicz's turbulent life.

61. http://www.rte.ie/centuryireland/index.php/articles/james-connolly-what-should-irish-people-do-during-the-war

62. www.marxists.org/archive/connolly/1916/02/slums.htm

63. http://www.sligoheritage.com/archmark2.htm gives a sympathetic account of Con's involvement with the Uprising

64. http://www.sligoheritage.com/archmark2.html

65. http://www.sligoheritage.com/archmark2.html

66. http://www.sligoheritage.com/archmark2.html

67. For Makievicz's Collected letters see Anne Haverty *Irish Revolutionary*; Virago Press *Prison Letters of Countess Markievicz*

68. jwa.org/encyclopedia/article/rothschild-constance-lady-battersea

69. See, 'Russell, Adeline Mary, duchess of Bedford (1852–1920)', *Oxford Dictionary of National Biography*,]

70. Mitchell p. 360

71. Mitchell p. 360

72. Mitchell p. 361

73. Mitchell p. 364

74. Sean O'Casey, *Mirror in My House: The Autobiographies* p. 316

**Chapter Three: 'Deeds not Words'**

1. See *inter alia* Anita Anand *Sophia: Princess, Suffragette, Revolutionary* p. 247

2. Anand p. 248

3. Lady Rhondda *My World* p. 90

4. See Rosen *Rise Up Women* pp. 138-142

5. Deposition given to Dr Flora Murray and quoted in Rosen p. 139

6. *Votes for Women* 25 November 1910

7. Katherine Connelly 'The Suffragettes, Black Friday and two types of window smashing'. Counterfire. 18/11/2010. For Ada Wright see Crawford *The Women's Suffrage Movement*

8. For Cecelia Haig's death see Lady Rhondda p. 90

9. ed. Joyce Marlow *Suffragettes* and Anand provide many examples of depositions.

10. *The Times* 11 March 1911

11. See Crawford p. 13

12. See trove.nla.gov.au

13. Quoted in Amanda Markwell 'Louisa Garrett Anderson Suffrage Prisoner' in *Women's History Network* February 2016

14. J. F. Geddes (2009) 'The Doctors' Dilemma: medical women and the British suffrage movement, *Women's History Review*, 18:2, 203-218 p. 210

15. See Crawford p. 13

16. See J. F. Geddes (2008) 'Culpable Complicity: the medical profession and the forcible feeding of suffragettes, 1909–1914', Women's History Review, 17:1, 79-94, fn 25

17. Flora Murray *Women as Army Surgeons: Being the History of the Women's Hospital Corps in Paris, Wimereux and Endell Street, September 1914–October 1919* p. 3-4

18. Murray p. 24-25

19. Murray p. 29

20. Murray p. 54

21. Murray p. 56

22. *British Medical Journal* 1914, **ii**: 767

23. Letters 22 and 27 September 1914

24. Murray p. 57

25. Evelyn Sharp, *Unfinished adventure: selected reminiscences from an Englishwoman's life*, p. 160

26. Sharp p. 160

27. Sharp p. 160

28. Murray p. 96

29. Murray p. 100

30. Murray p. 111

31. Murray. p. 113

32. Murray p. 129

33. See J. F. Geddes (2009) 'The Doctors' Dilemma: medical women and the British suffrage movement', *Women's History Review*, 18:2, 203-218, p. 206

34. See Brian Harrison, 'Women's health and the women's movement in Britain: 1840–1940', in Charles Webster (ed.), *Biology, medicine and society 1840–1940*, Cambridge University Press, 1981, pp. 15–72, p. 51

35. Murray p. 156

36. Murray p. 156

37. Murray p. 134

38. Murray p. 134

39. See www.drsusancohen.wordpress.com/2014/06/01/forgotten-women-surgeons-the-work-of-the-womens-hospital-corps-in-the-first-world-war

40. Murray p. 139
41. Murray p. 166
42. See https://womanandhersphere.com/tag/flora-murray
43. Crawford p. 279
44. For Vera Scantlebury see Jennian F Geddes 'Deeds *and* Words in the Suffrage Military Hospital in Endell Street' *Medical History*. 2007 Jan 1; 51(1): 79–98.
45. Murray p. 181
46. Murray p. 209
47. See Murray p. 240
48. Murray p. 241
49. Murray p. 262
50. See Geddes 'Deeds and Words'
51. See Geddes 'Artistic Integrity and a Spat at the Endell Street Military Hospital' in *The Burlington Magazine*, Vol. 147, No. 1230, Painting in England (Sep., 2005), pp.617-618
52. See http://discovery.ucl.ac.uk/1383587/1/412336.pdf
53. Marchioness of Londonderry *Retrospect* Muller, London, 1938 p. 127
54. Anne de Courcy *Society's Queen: The Life of Edith, Marchioness of Londonderry* p. 98
55. Londonderry p. 104
56. Significant excerpts from the tract can be read on http://www.historyofwomen.org/antiwright.html
57. Londonderry *Retrospect* p. 105. Savill worked with the SWH at Royaumont.
58. de Courcy p. 108
59. Londonderry p. 76
60. de Courcy p. 108
61. Londonderry p. 127.
62. Londonderry p. 127
63. Jennifer Gould PhD thesis available at http://discovery.ucl.ac.uk/1317607/1/260868.pdf p. 35
64. See Londonderry p. 112-113 and de Courcy p. 132
65. de Courcy p. 132-3
66. de Courcy p. 134
67. See Chapter 2
68. de Courcy p. 135 and *The Times* 24 November 1910
69. Londonderry p. 110

70. Elizabeth Gore *The Better Fight* p. 62; Londonderry p. 118

71. Gore p. 63

72. *Clarence and Richmond Examiner* NSW 8 September 1908; John Bullock *Fast Women: The Drivers Who Changed the Face of Motor Racing* p. 32

73. Londonderry p. 123

74. Londonderry p. 134

75. Londonderry p. 125

76. See   http://womenslegionmotordrivers1919photos.blogspot.co.uk/2008/05/newly-discovered-scrapbook-belonging-to.html

77. de Courcy p. 159

78. See Londonderry 127 and Lady Londonderry *Woman's Indirect Influence and its Effect on Character: Her Position improved by the Franchise Morally and Materially* 1919

79. IWM WWC, Army 12/5 Interview with Mrs Chalmers Watson

80. Molly Izzard *A Heroine in her Time: A Life of Dame Helen Gwynne-Vaughan* p. 106

81. Her uncle was the Scottish peer Lord Saltoun and for a while it seemed that she might inherit the title

82. Izzard p. 83

83. Izzard p. 129

84. Helen Gwynne-Vaughan *Service with the Army* p. 13

85. Philo-Gill p. 3

86. Roy Terry *Women in Khaki* p. 25; Lucy Noakes *Women in the British Army: War and the Gentle Sex, 1907–1948*

87. IWM WWC, Army 3 6/3 *Minute to Lord Derby re Conference for Women*

88. TNA Ministry of National Service (NATS) 1/1271 Letter from Women's Interest Committee of the NUWSS 26/01/17 also quoted in Philo-Gill p. 166

89. Gould p. 147

90. Izzard p. 133

91. Gwynne-Vaughan p. 18

92. Gwynne-Vaughan p. 15

93. Gwynne-Vaughan p. 18

94. IWM Sound Archive Cat No. 44

95. See B[ritish] E[mpire] U[nion]. Monthly Record November 1917.

96. *Daily Sketch* 20 February 1918 See also *The Times* 11 February 1918

97. See Roy Terry, 'Watson, Alexandra Mary Chalmers (1872–1936)' http://dx.doi.org/10.1093/ref:odnb/67666

98. Gwynne–Vaughan p. 67
99. Gwynne–Vaughan p. 67
100. Quoted in Terry p. 112

**Chapter Four: 'Votes for Women'? No Thanks!**

1. Julia Bush *Women Against the Vote* p. 2. The other key anti-suffrage text is Brian Harrison *Separate Spheres: The Opposition to Women's Suffrage in Britain*
2. Harrison, p. 118
3. See Harrison p. 118
4. Bush p. 28
5. Bush p. 4
6. Strachey p. 319
7. Smith p. 23
8. See Crawford *Reference Guide*
9. Fawcett p. 79
10. Harrison p. 153
11. *Women's National Anti-Suffrage League* leaflet 12 quoted in Bush p. 82
12. Harrison, p. 134
13. *Common Cause* 7 March 1912 p. 818
14. *Anti-Suffrage Review* July 1914 p. 110
15. See Harrison p. 182
16. See Harrison p. 199
17. See Bush p. 257
18. See http://www.radionz.co.nz/national/programmes/ninetonoon/audio/20146055/jane-tolerton-on-the-role-women-played-in-the-first-world-war; http://www.rouen-histoire.com/14-18/Hopital_Bonsecours.htm; *Evening Post*, Volume LXXXIX, Issue 60, 12 March 1915 For anti-suffragists at Royaumont See Jennian Geddes 'The Doctor's Dilemma' fn 54
19. See Harrison p. 206
20. Strachey p. 355
21. See Sutherland p. 351
22. Mrs Humphry Ward 'The Women's Anti-Suffrage Movement' *Nineteenth Century* 64, August 1908 pp. 343-352 p. 342; 'Some Suffragist Arguments' *Educational Review* 36, pp. 398–404 p. 399
23. See Sutherland p. 299
24. See Crawford p. 99 There is no hint that Ward dismissed her.

25. Sunderland pp. 215-229, p. 350
26. Maroula Joannou 'Mary Augusta Ward (Mrs Humphry) and the Opposition to Women's Suffrage' *Women's History Review, Volume 14, Numbers 3&4, 2005* pp. 561-579 p. 562
27. Quoted in Joannou p. 563
28. *The Times* 27 February 1909
29. Sunderland p. 302-3
30. See Sunderland p. 303
31. Sutherland p. 352
32. Letter 6
33. *England's Effort (EE)* p. 7
34. Letters 3 and 4
35. Sutherland p. 354 and *EE* Letter 6
36. *Towards the Goal* Letter 2
37. See Sutherland p. 362
38. Sutherland p. 363
39. For example *Fields of Victory* Letter 1
40. Sutherland p. 370
41. Sutherland p. 371
42. For information about this see http://www.marywardcentre.ac.uk
43. Bush p. 2
44. Harrison p. 131; Letter 13 July 1913
45. See Harrison p. 164
46. Brian Blakeley 'The Society for the Oversea Settlement of British Women and the Problems of Empire Settlement, 1917-1936' *Albion: A Quarterly Journal Concerned with British Studies, Vol. 20, No. 3 (Autumn, 1988)*, pp. 421-444 p. 442
47. Quoted in Martin Pugh, 'Pott, Gladys Sydney (1867–1961)', Oxford Dictionary of National Biography, Oxford University Press, 2004 [http://www.oxforddnb.com/view/article/41259]
48. Harrison p. 189
49. Harrison p. 184
50. See Crawford p. 111
51. Harrison p. 113
52. Harrison p. 175
53. See *The Times* 2 October 1917. Nicola Verdon 'Left out in the Cold: Village Women and Agricultural Labour in England and Wales during the First World

War' *Twentieth Century British History, Vol. 27, No. 1*, 2016, pp. 1–25. The WLA probably made up c. 5 per cent of the agricultural labour force, 'village women' 25 per cent

54. *Daily Record* 31 August 1914
55. Verdon p. 7
56. See http://www.surreyinthegreatwar.org.uk/story/sarah-boyces-diary-24th-february-5th-march-1916 for Boyse's diary
57. *Reading Mercury* 8 April 1916
58. *Reading Mercury* 11 March 1916
59. Verdon p. 21
60. See Mrs Usborne *Women's* Work in *Wartime A Handbook of Employment* 1917 p. 122 and Gladys Pott 'Women in Agriculture' in Usborne p. 117
61. Usborne p. 125
62. See amongst many others *Banbury Guardian* 8 June 1918
63. Blakeley p. 432
64. See Blakely p. 444
65. Millicent Fawcett in a Reply to Mary Ward's Appeal published in *Nineteenth Century* June 1889 and widely quoted in suffrage historiography
66. *Nottingham Evening Post* 6 November 1908
67. *Derbyshire Daily Telegraph* 7 November 1908
68. See Eliza Reidi 'Options for an Imperialist Woman: The Case of Violet Markham 1899-1914' in *Albion: A Quarterly Journal Concerned with British Studies*, Vol. 32, No. 1(Spring, 2000), pp. 59-84 p. 80
69. Violet Markham *Return Passage* p. 97
70. David Mitchell *The Fighting Pankhursts* p. 322
71. Markham to Cromer, 10 December 1913, Cromer papers, F0633/22/207, PRO
72. See Reidi p. 81
73. *The Times* 26 March 1915
74. See Reizi pp 81-2
75. See Alan Simmonds *Britain and World War One* p. 57
76. Markham p. 147 and ff for this 'fiasco'.
77. Markham p. 154
78. Markham p. 155
79. Markham p. 155
80. Markham p. 157

81. See Liora Lukitz *A Quest in the Middle East: Gertrude Bell and the Making of Modern Iraq* p. 47

82. Janet Wallach *Desert Queen* p. 82 (no source given) but see Lady Bell *Selected Letters of Gertrude Bell* p. 215

83. Georgina Howell *Daughter of the Desert* p. 76

84. Newcastle University Gertrude Bell Archive

85. Wallach p. 92

86. Wallach p. 133

87. See Wallach p. 134

88. Wallach 135

89. http://www.civilservant.org.uk/women-gertrude_bell.html

90. 14 April 1915 letter to Charles Doughty-Wylie http://www.gerty.ncl.ac.uk/letter_details.php?letter_id=1846

91. Wallach p. 145

92. Wallach p. 160

93. See Howell p. 307

94. Florence Bell p. 349, p. 373

95. Bell p. 377

96. Howell p. 382

97. Howell p. 396

98. Wallach p. 373

99. Bell p. 624

100. http://hansard.millbanksystems.com/commons/1926/jul/14/miss-gertrude-bell#S5CV0198P0_19260714_HOC_242

101. Wallach p. 377

**Chapter Five: 'I tried to stop the bloody thing!'**

1. Crawford p. 301

2. Anne Wiltsher *Most Dangerous Women* p. 13

3. Wiltsher p. 13

4. See Wiltsher p. 20

5. 'International manifesto of Women' published in *Votes for Women* 7 August 1914

6. Wiltsher p. 23

7. Mrs St Clair Stobart *The Flaming Sword in Serbia* p. 147

8. Wiltsher p. 24

9. *Common Cause* 14 August 1914

10. *Manchester Courier* 9 September 1914

11. Harold Smith p. 97

12. See Jo Vellacott *Patriots, Pacifists and the Vote* p. 72 & 77

13. Wiltsher p. 72

14. Sylvia Pankhurst *The Home Front (HF)* p. 149

15. Wiltsher p. 84; Sheila Fletcher *Maude Royden: A Life* p. 124

16. Hochschild p. 140

17. See L.B. Costin 'Feminism, pacifism, internationalism and the 1915 international congress of women' *Women's Studies International Forum*, Volume 5 (3/4), 1982

18. See Pankhurst *Home Front* p. xii

19. *The Times* 9 September 1914

20. E. S. Pankhurst, *The Suffragette Movement*, p.517

21. June Hannam, 'Pankhurst, (Estelle) Sylvia (1882–1960)', *Oxford Dictionary of National Biography*, Oxford University Press, 2004; online edn, Sept 2015 [http://www.oxforddnb.com/view/article/37833,]

22. Pankhurst p. 25

23. See Pankhurst p. 25

24. Pankhurst p. 80-1

25. Pankhurst p. 78

26. Pankhurst p. 47

27. Pankhurst p. 53

28. Stanislav Tumis 'The British Women's Peace Movement during World War 1 p. 313 in *The Czech Lands in the Midst of Europe in the Past and Today*. p. 316

29. *Western Daily Press* 9 December 1916

30. Barbara Winslow *Sylvia Pankhurst: Sexual Politics And Political Activism* p. 85

31. Wiltsher p. 143

32. 18 December 1916

33. Hochschild p. 315

34. *Derby Daily Telegraph* 29 October 1918

35. Frank Briant, Lambeth Board of Guardians 1898

36. http://www.menwhosaidno.org/context/women/dsespard_c.html

37. Hochschild p. 14-15

38. Hochschild p. 15

39. Margaret Mulvihill *Charlotte Despard* p. 64

40. Mulvihill p. 73

41. Charlotte Despard 'Why I became a "suffragette"', *Women's Franchise* (4 July 1907)
42. See Mulvihill p. 74
43. Crawford p. 168
44. Mulvihill p. 103
45. Mulvihill p. 115
46. http://www.menwhosaidno.org/context/women/dsespard_c.html
47. http://www.menwhosaidno.org/context/women/womens_peace_crusade.html
48. Stanislav Tumis 'The British Women's Peace Movement during World War 1 xin *The Czech Lands in the Midst of Europe in the Past and Today.* p. 313
49. Crawford p. 611
50. *The Times* 31 July 1956
51. Fletcher *Maude Royden: A Life* p. 123-124
52. See Wiltsher p. 137
53. Fletcher p. 132
54. Peter Street https://womenandthechurch.org/resources/maude-royden-1876-1956/
55. See Vivien Newman *Tumult and Tears* p. 49-50
56. Street
57. See Street
58. Fletcher p. 133
59. *Church Times* 'A life spent battling for women' 2 November 2006
60. See for example *The Chronicle* 17 March 1917
61. *Sheffield Daily Telegraph and Post* 19 September 1917
62. *Chester Chronicle* 16 February 1918
63. *The Chronicle* 16 February 1918
64. *Daily Mirror* 27 May 1918
65. *The Herald* 30 March 1918
66. *Liverpool Echo* 20 September 1918
67. See Trevor Beeson *The Church's Other Half: Women's Ministry* p. 134 ff
68. Beeson p. 135
69. Kate Adie *Fighting on the Home Front* p. 233
70. Jennifer Hobhouse Balme *Agent of Peace Emily Hobhouse* p. 15
71. Hochschild p. 35
72. See Balme p. 13-14

73. Vellacott p. 76

74. Hobhouse 'Open Christmas Letter' widely available on internet.

75. Balme p. 29 & 44

76. See Larry Zuckermann *The Rape of Belgium: The Untold Story of World War I*

77. Balme p. 89

78. Hochschild p. 219

79. http://hansard.millbanksystems.com/commons/1916/oct/31/miss-emily-hobhouse-passport

80. Balme p. 136

81. See Chris Northcott *MI5 at War 1909–1918: How MI5 Foiled the Spies of the Kaiser in the First World War* p. 187-8

82. Hochschild p. 220

**Chapter Six: At No Cost to the Government**

1. https://blogs.loc.gov/law/2013/08/no-taxation-without-representation-circa-1215-ad-or-magna-carta-a-beginners-guide/

2. www.marxists.org/archive/montefiore/1925/autobiography/07.htm

3. *Western Daily Press* 10 November 1910

4. *Bucks Herald* 20 April 1912

5. Evelyn Sharp *Unfinished Adventure: Selected Reminiscences from an Englishwoman's Life* Chap 9

6. http://www.heretical.com/suffrage/1912pank.html

7. http://www.heretical.com/suffrage/1912pank.html

8. http://womenwhoroared.blogspot.fr/2014/01/millicent-fawcett-1847-1929.html

9. *Daily News* 9 March 1912

10. See Jane Chapman 'The Argument of the Broken Pane' *Media History*, 21:3, 238-251 p. 240 & 244

11. Chapman p. 245

12. Rosen *Rise Up Women!* p. 183-184

13. Mackworth p. 152

14. http://www.walesartsreview.org/commemoration-lady-rhondda-a-survivors-tale/

15. See *Derby Daily Telegraph* 11 June 1913

16. Lena Ashwell *Myself a Player (MAP)* p. 169

17. Ashwell *(MAP)* p. 170

18. Ashwell *(MAP)*p. 195
19. Lena Ashwell *Modern Troubadours (MT)* p. 5
20. Ashwell *MT* p. 7
21. ww.telegraph.co.uk/women/womens-life/11006714/WW1-centenary-Lena-Ashwell-parties-Shining-a-light-on-the-young-women-who-brought-music-to-the-trenches.html
22. Margaret Leask *Lena Ashwell Actress Patriot Pioneer* p. 119
23. Leask p.125
24. Siegfried Sassoon 'Concert Party' in *MT* p. 93
25. Ashwell *MT* p. 32
26. Ashwell *MT* p. 63
27. Ashwell *MAP* p. 204
28. Ashwell *MT* p. 115
29. *Sketch* 21 November 1917
30. Ashwell *MT* pp. 117-118
31. Ashwell *MAP* p. 20.
32. Ashwell *MAP* p. 206
33. *Boston Post* 11 April 1916
34. *Western Daily News* 24 September 1914
35. Monica Krippner *The Quality of Mercy* p. 38
36. *West London Press* 6 August 1915
37. Burke file, SWH collection, Mitchell Library, Glasgow
38. *Nottingham Journal* 5 February 1916 (Serbia has indeed not forgotten British women's contribution honouring them in an annual remembrance ceremony held in Nis on 14 February)
39. *Tablet* 2 March 1918
40. *Aberdeen Weekly Journal* 25 August 1916
41. Burke file, Glasgow.
42. See www.scarletfinders.co.uk diary 5 January 1918
43. Boyce Gaddes, *Evelina Haverfield* p. 41
44. Crawford p. 279
45. Annand p. 252-253
46. See for example *Yorkshire Telegraph* 23 November 1910
47. Gaddes pp. 61, 65
48. Krippner p. 73
49. See Boyce p. 95

50. Margaret Lawrence *Shadow of Swords* p. 21

51. See Cahill *Between the Lines* p. 55

52. Lawrence p. 218

53. Isobel Hutton *With a Woman's Unit in Serbia* p. 225

54. Lawrence p. 119

55. *The Times* 20 June 1913

56. www.lucienneboyce.com/wp-content/uploads/2016/07/A-Womens-Suffrage-Timeline.pdf

57. See Jane Conway *A Woman of Two Wars* p. 41ff

58. Conway p. 47

59. *Brooklyn Life* p. 18

60. Conway p. 65

61. Mary Borden in Newman p. 142

62. Conway p. 76

63. Borden 'Come to Me Quickly' in ed. O'Prey *Poems of Love and War* p. 41

64. Conway p. 95

**Conclusion: Dreams (Un)fulfilled**

1. Harold Smith *The British Women's Suffrage Campaign 1866–1928* p. 99

2. Smith p. 100

3. See Sharp

4. 'The Vote' February 1918

5. Marlow *Suffragettes* p. 246

6. *Workers' Dreadnought* 16 February 1918

7. Smith p. 100

8. Smith p. 101

9. https://core.ac.uk/download/pdf/43950.pdf

10. *Western Gazette* 18 November 1927

11. *Northern Whig and Belfast Post* 15 July 1927

12. *Aberdeen Press and Journal* 18 July 1927

13. My thanks to Capt. C Earl for this information

14. www.bma.org.uk/news/2016/april/contract-will-have-adverse-effect-on-women August 2017

15. *Fawcett Society* 24 August 201

# Select Bibliography

Adie, Kate, *Fighting on the Home Front*, Hodder, 2014

Allen, Mary, *Lady in Blue* Chatto and Windus, 1936

Allen, Mary, *The Pioneer Policewoman* Chatto and Windus, 1925

Anand, Anita, *Sophia: Princess, Suffragette, Revolutionary*, Bloomsbury, 2015

Ashwell, Lena, *Modern Troubadours* Glydendal, 1922

Ashwell, Lena, *Myself A Player* Michael Joseph, 1936

Atkinson, Diane, *The Suffragettes in Pictures* Sutton, 1996

Balfour, Betty, ed., *Letters of Lady Constance Lytton* Heinemann, 1925

Balme, Jennifer Hobhouse, *Agent of Peace Emily Hobhouse* History Press, 2015

Bartley Paula, *Votes for Women* Hodder, 2011

Bates, Stephen *Asquith Haus, 2006*

Beeson, Trevor, *The Church's Other Half: Women's Ministry* SCM, 2011

Bell, Lady ed., *Selected Letters of Gertrude Bell* Benn, 1930

Boyd, Nina *From Suffragette to Fascist: The Many Lives of Mary Sophia Allen* History Press, 2013

*British Medical Journal* 1914, ii

Brittain, Vera, *Testament of Youth* Virago, 1985

Burke, Kathleen, *The White Road to Verdun* Hodder & Stoughton, 1916

Burnham, Karyn, *The Courage of Cowards* Pen & Sword, 2014

Bush, Julia, *Women Against the Vote*, 2007

Cahill, Audrey, *Between the Lines* Pentland Press, 1992

Carrier, John, (1973) 'The Control of women by women: The Women Police', *The Society for the Study of Labour History* 26

Conway, Jane, *A Woman of Two Wars* Munday, 2010

Crawford, Elizabeth ed., *Campaigning for the Vote Kate Frye's Suffrage Diary* Francis Boutle, 2013

Crawford, Elizabeth, *The Women's Suffrage Movement* Routledge, 2001 de Courcy, Anne, *Society's Queen: The Life of Edith, Marchioness of Londonderry* W&N, 2004

Fawcett, Millicent Garrett, *The Women's Victory and After 1911-1918*, Cambridge, 1920

Fletcher, Sheila, *Maude Royden: A Life* Basil Blackwell, 1989

Gaddes, Boyce, *Evelina Haverfield* Braunton, 1995

Gore, Elizabeth, *The Better Fight: The Story of Dame Elizabeth Barker*, Bles, 1965

Gould, Jennifer, PhD thesis 'The Women's Corps: The Establishment of Women's Military Service in Britain', 1988

Gwynne-Vaughan, Helen, *Service with the Army* Hutchinson n.d.

Hamilton, Cicely, *A Pageant of Great Women* 1910, Marion Lawson, 1948

Harrison Brian, *Separate Spheres: The Opposition to Women's Suffrage in Britain* Croom, Helm, 1978

Harrison Brian, 'Women's health and the women's movement in Britain: 1840–1940', in Charles Webster (ed.), *Biology, medicine and society 1840–1940*, Cambridge University Press, 1981

Haverty, Anne, *Irish Revolutionary*; *Prison Letters of Countess Markievicz* Virago, 1987

Hochschild, Adam, *To End All Wars: How the First World War Divided Britain*, Harcourt, 2011

Howell, Georgina, *Daughter of the Desert* Pan Macmillan, 2006

Hume, Leslie Parker, *The National Union of Women's Suffrage Societies 1897–1914*, Garland, 1982

Hutton, Isobel, *With a Woman's Unit in Serbia* Williams, 1928

Izzard, Molly, *A Heroine in her Time: A Life of Dame Helen Gwynne-Vaughan,* Macmillan, 1969

Krippner, Monica, *The Quality of Mercy* David & Charles, 1980

Lawrence, Margaret, *Shadow of Swords* Michael Joseph, 1971

Leask, Margaret, *Lena Ashwell Actress Patriot Pioneer* University of Hertfordshire, 2012

Lock, Joan, *The British Policewoman her Story* Hale, 1978

Londonderry, Lady, *Woman's Indirect Influence and its Effect on Character: Her Position improved by the Franchise Morally and Materially,* 1919

Londonderry, Marchioness of, *Retrospect* Muller, 1938

Lukitz Liora, *A Quest in the Middle East: Gertrude Bell and the Making of Modern Iraq* I. B. Taurus, 2006

Markham, Violet, *Return Passage* OUP, 1953

Marlow, Joyce ed., *Suffragettes* Virago, 2000

Marwick, Arthur, *Women at War* Croom, Helm, 1977

Mitchell, David, *The Fighting Pankhursts* Macmillan, 1967

Mitchell, David, *Women on the Warpath* Davidson, 1997

Mulvihill, Margaret, *Charlotte Despard* Pandora, 1989

Murray, Flora, *Women as Army Surgeons: Being the History of the Women's Hospital Corps in Paris, Wimereux and Endell Street, September 1914 – October 1919* Hodder & Stoughton, n.d.

Newman, Vivien, *Tumult & Tears* Pen & Sword, 2016

Noakes, Lucy, *Women in the British Army: War and the Gentle Sex, 1907–1948* Routledge, 2006

Northcott, Chris, *MI5 at War 1909–1918* Tattered Flag, 2015

O'Prey, Paul ed., *Poems of Love and War* Dare-Gale, 2015

O'Casey, Sean, *Mirror in My House: The Autobiographies* Macmillan, 1956

Pankhurst, Sylvia, *The Home Front* Cresset 1987

Pankhurst, E.S., *The Suffragette Movement*, Virago, 1984

Philo-Gill, Samantha, *The Women's Auxiliary Corps in France 1917–1921*, Pen & Sword, 2017

Pugh, Martin, *Women's Suffrage in Britain, 1867–1928* Historical Association, 1980

Rhondda, Lady (Margaret Mackworth), *This Was My World* Macmillan, 1933

Rippon, Nicola, *The Plot to Kill Lloyd George: The Story of Alice Wheeldon and the Peartree Conspiracy* Wharncliffe, 2009

Rosen, Michael, *Rise Up Women* Routledge, 1974

Rowbotham, Sylvia, *Friends of Alice Wheeldon* Pluto Press, 1986

Sharp, Evelyn, *Unfinished adventure: selected reminiscences from an Englishwoman's life,* Faber, 1933

Sigillito, Gina, *Daughters of Maeve: 50 Irish Women Who Changed the World*, Citadel, 2007

Simmonds, Alan, *Britain and World War One* Routledge, 2011

Smith, Harold, *The British Women's Suffrage Campaign 1866–1928*, Routledge, 2009

Stokes, Michelle, PhD Thesis 'A Measure of the Elite: A History of Medical Practitioners in Harley Street', 2004

Storr Katherine, *Excluded from the Record Women Refugees and Relief 1914–1929* Lang, 2009

Strachey, Ray, *The Cause*, Virago, 1988

Street, Peter, https://womenandthechurch.org/resources/maude-royden-1876-1956/

Sutherland, John, *Mrs Humphrey Ward Eminent Victorian, Pre-eminent Edwardian*, Clarendon, 1990

Terry, Roy, *Women in Khaki* Columbus, 1988

Thom, Deborah, *Nice Girls and Rude Girls Women Workers in World War One* I. B. Taurus, 1998

Thomson, Basil, *The Story of Scotland Yard* Literary Guild, 1935

Tickner, Lisa, *The Spectacle of Women: Imagery of the Suffrage Campaign 1907–1914* University of Chicago Press, 1988

Usborne, Mrs, *Women's* Work *in Wartime A Handbook of Employment* 1917

Vellacott, Jo, *Patriots, Pacifists and the Vote* Palgrave, 2007

Wallach, Janet, *Desert Queen* Penguin, 1996

Ward, Mary, *England's Effort* Smith Elder, 1916

Ward, Mary, *Fields of Victory*, Hutchinson, 1919

Ward, Mary, *Towards the Goal* John Murray, 1917

Wiltsher, Anne, *Most Dangerous Women* Pandora, 1985

Winslow, Barbara, *Sylvia Pankhurst: Sexual Politics And Political Activism* UCL Press, 1996

Zuckermann, Larry, *The Rape of Belgium: The Untold Story of World War I* NYUP, 2004

## Articles

Blakeley, Brian, 'The Society for the Oversea Settlement of British Women and the Problems of Empire Settlement, 1917–1936' *Albion: A Quarterly Journal Concerned with British Studies, Vol. 20, No. 3 (Autumn, 1988)*, pp. 421-444

*British Medical Journal* 1914, ii

Chapman, Jane, 'The Argument of the Broken Pane' in *Media History*, 21:3, 238-251

*Church Times*, 'A life spent battling for women' 2 November 2006

Connelly, Katherine, 'The Suffragettes, Black Friday and two types of window smashing'. http://www.counterfire.org/articles/75-our-history/7697-the-suffragettes-black-friday-and-the-two-types-of-window-smashing *Counterfire*. 18/11/2010.

Costin, L. B., 'Feminism, pacifism, internationalism and the 1915 international congress of women' *Women's Studies International Forum*, Volume 5 (3/4), 1982

Despard, Charlotte, 'Why I became a "suffragette"', *Women's Franchise* (4 July 1907)

Faraut, Martine, Women resisting the vote: a case of anti feminism?, *Women's History Review*, (2003) 12:4, 605-621

Geddes, 'J. F., Artistic Integrity and a Spat at the Endell Street Military Hospital' in *The Burlington Magazine*, Vol. 147, No. 1230, Painting in England (Sep., 2005),

Geddes, J. F., (2008) 'Culpable Complicity: the medical profession and the forcible feeding of suffragettes, 1909–1914', Women's History Review, 17:1, 79-94

Geddes, J. F., (2009) 'The Doctors' Dilemma: medical women and the British suffrage movement', *Women's History Review*, 18:2, 203-218

Harman, William, 'The Forcible Feeding Of Suffrage Prisoners' *The Lancet* 180, No. 4644, p. 671–672, 31 August 1912

Hiley, Nicholas, 'Internal Security in Wartime: The Rise and Fall of PMS2, 1915 – 1917', *Intelligence and National Security*, 1986, vol. 1, issue 3.

Jackson, John, 'Alice Wheeldon and the Attorney-General; in 'Losing the Plot: Lloyd George, F. E. Smith and the trial of Alice Wheeldon', *History Today*, 2007

Joannou, Maroula, 'Mary Augusta Ward (Mrs Humphry) and the Opposition to Women's Suffrage' *Women's History Review, Volume 14, Numbers 3&4, 2005* pp. 561-579

Levine, P. '"Walking the streets in a way no decent woman should": Women police in World War I', *Journal of Modern History*, 66 (1994), 34–78

Markwell, Amanda, 'Louisa Garrett Anderson Suffrage Prisoner' *Women's History Network* February 2016

Mrs Humphry Ward, 'The Women's Anti-Suffrage Movement' *Nineteenth Century* 64, August, 1908 pp. 343-352

Mrs Humphry Ward, 'Some Suffragist Arguments' *Educational Review* 36, (1908) pp. 398–404

Reidi, Eliza 'Options for an Imperialist Woman: The Case of Violet Markham 1899–1914' in *Albion: A Quarterly Journal Concerned with British Studies*, Vol. 32, No. 1(Spring, 2000), pp. 59-84

Tumis, Stanislav, 'The British Women's Peace Movement during World War I. A Contribution towards the Study of British Appeasement' in: *Prague papers on History of International Relations* Praha: Institute of World History (2009), pp. 309-324

Turner, Edmund, *The American Political Science Review*, Vol. 7, No. 4 (Nov., 1913), pp. 588-609 Published by: American Political Science Association

Verdon, Nicola, 'Left out in the Cold: Village Women and Agricultural Labour in England and Wales during the First World War' *Twentieth Century British History, Vol. 27, No. 1*, 2016, pp. 1–25

Woodeson, Alison, (1993) 'The first women police: a force for equality or infringement?', *Women's History Review*, 2:2, pp. 217–32.

## Websites (Accessed April–August 2017):

blogs.loc.gov/law/2013/08/no-taxation-without-representation-circa-1215-ad-or-magna-carta-a-beginners-guide/

hansard.millbanksystems.com/commons/1916/oct/31/miss-emily-hobhouse-passport

metro.co.uk/2016/06/14/emmeline-pankhurst-suffragette-who-helped-give-women-the-vote-5942418

womenshistorynetwork.org/excluded-from-the-record-women-refugees-and-relief-1914-1929

www.bma.org.uk/news/2016/april/contract-will-have-adverse-effect-on-women

www.core.ac.uk/download/pdf/43950

www.civilservant.org.uk/women-gertrude_bell.html

www.derbyshirelife.co.uk/out-about/places/the-village-of-breadsall-derbyshire-1-1630424

www.derbyshirelife.co.uk/out-about/places/the-village-of-breadsall-derbyshire-1-1630424

www.drsusancohen.wordpress.com/2014/06/01/forgotten-women-surgeons-the-work-of-the-womens-hospital-corps-in-the-first-world-war

www.gerty.ncl.ac.uk/letter_details.php?letter_id=1846

www.heanorhistory.org.uk/suffragettes.html

www.heretical.com/suffrage/1912pank.html

www.historicalpageants.ac.uk/featured-pageants/sherborne-pageant-1905/

www.historyofwomen.org/antiwright.html

www.jwa.org/encyclopedia/article/rothschild-constance-lady-battersea

www.lucienneboyce.com/wp-content/uploads/2016/07/A-Womens-Suffrage-Timeline

www.marxists.org/archive/connolly/1916/02/slums.htm

www.marxists.org/archive/montefiore/1925/autobiography/07

www.menwhosaidno.org/context/women/womens_peace_crusade.html

www.nytimes.com/interactive/2017/01/22/us/politics/womens-march-trump-crowd-estimates.html

www.theguardian.com/us-news/2017/jan/21/donald-trump-first-24-hours-global-protests-dark-speech-healthcare

www.oxforddoddnb.com

www.radionz.co.nz/national/programmes/ninetonoon/audio/20146055/jane-tolerton-on-the-role-women-played-in-the-first-world-war; http://www.rouen-histoire.com/14-18/Hopital_Bonsecours.htm;

www.rte.ie/centuryireland/index.php/articles/james-connolly-what-should-irish-people-do-during-the-war

www.rte.ie/centuryireland/index.php/articles/james-connolly-what-should-irish-people-do-during-the-war

www.sheroesofhistory.wordpress.com/2015/09/03/katherine-harley

www.sligoheritage.com/archmark2.htm

www.surreyinthegreatwar.org.uk/story/sarah-boyces-diary-24th-february-5th-march-1916

www.telegraph.co.uk/women/womens-life/11006714/WW1-centenary-Lena-Ashwell-parties-Shining-a-light-on-the-young-women-who-brought-music-to-the-trenches

www.walesartsreview.org/commemoration-lady-rhondda-a-survivors-tale

www.womanandhersphere.com/tag/flora-murray

www.womenslegionmotordrivers1919photos.blogspot.co.uk/2008/05/newly-discovered-scrapbook-belonging-to.html

www.womenwhoroared.blogspot.fr/2014/01/millicent-fawcett-1847-1929.html

# Index